**VOTES OF
CONFIDENCE**
2ND EDITION

✓OTES OF CONFIDENCE

A YOUNG PERSON'S GUIDE TO AMERICAN ELECTIONS

JEFF FLEISCHER

2ND EDITION

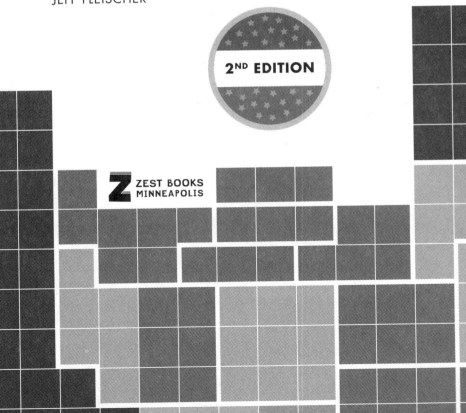

Z ZEST BOOKS
MINNEAPOLIS

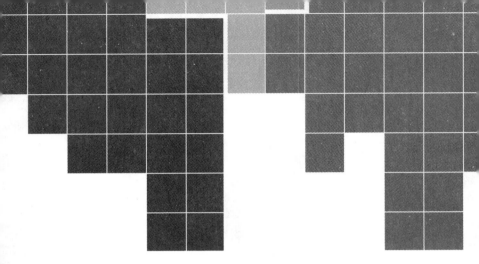

Zest Books™
An imprint of Lerner Publishing Group, Inc.
241 First Avenue North
Minneapolis, MN 55401 USA

For reading levels and more information, look up this title
at www.lernerbooks.com.
Visit us at zestbooks.net.

Main body text set in Adobe Caslon Pro.
Typeface provided by Adobe Systems.

Library of Congress Cataloging-in-Publication Data

Names: Fleischer, Jeff author.
Title: Votes of confidence: a young person's guide to American elections / by Jeff Fleischer.
Description: Second Edition, Updated Edition. | Minneapolis: Zest Books, [2020] | Audience: Ages: 11–18. | Audience: Grades: 9 to 12. | Previous edition published: San Francisco, California: Zest Books, [2016] under title Votes of Confidence. | Includes bibliographical references. | Identifiers: LCCN 2019013046 (print) | LCCN 2019014186 (ebook) | ISBN 9781541583887 (eb pdf) | ISBN 9781541578968 (library binding : alk. paper) | ISBN 9781541578975 (paperback : alk. paper) | ISBN 9781541583887 (eb pdf)
Subjects: LCSH: Elections—United States—Juvenile literature. | Representative government and representation—United States.
Classification: LCC JK1978 (ebook) | LCC JK1978 .F55 2020 (print) | DDC 324.60973—dc23

LC record available at https://lccn.loc.gov/2019013046

Manufactured in the United States of America
1-47087-47887-8/27/2019

CONTENTS

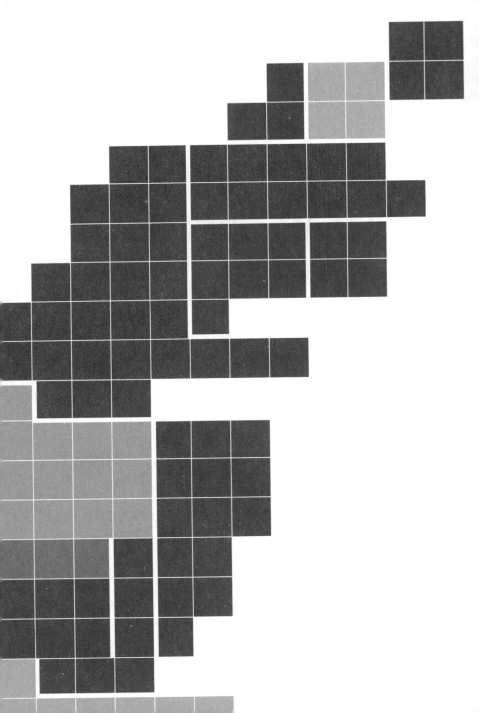

INTRODUCTION

When I wrote the first edition of *Votes of Confidence* in 2015, my goal was to create a handy primer for young voters about politics and elections, and one that could also serve as a refresher for older readers. By the time the book showed up in stores in May of 2016, the United States was in the middle of one of the craziest election cycles in the country's history.

The 2016 race featured a perfect storm of unusual circumstances. When Barack Obama won the presidency in 2008, it was the first time in more than five decades that neither the Democrats nor the Republicans had a sitting president or vice president running; just eight years later, the same thing happened. (Vice President Joe Biden would have been an obvious candidate, but he chose not to run after the untimely death of his son Beau.) The Democratic primaries ended with Hillary Clinton becoming the first woman to win a major American party's presidential nomination, after a close race against longtime independent Senator Bernie Sanders of Vermont, who fared particularly well among young voters. The Republican process saw more than a dozen governors and senators from across the country, and the most diverse group of candidates in GOP history, lose to Donald Trump, a business and TV celebrity who became the first president without either government or military experience, and who routinely used false information and conspiracy theories against both his Republican and Democratic opponents.

The country was therefore treated to the odd spectacle of a race to replace a still-young and popular president that featured two candidates a generation older and significantly less popular than him. The outcome was also bizarre, as the Democratic nominee won the nationwide popular vote for the sixth time in the past seven elections dating back to 1992 . . . but, because of the electoral vote, lost the election. About three million more voters backed Clinton, but a margin of fewer than one hundred thousand votes spread across three traditionally Democratic states meant that didn't matter.

Plenty of other factors led to an election that history classes will study for a long time.

The government of Russia carried out successful and unprecedented cyberattacks against the US election: hacking the Democratic National Committee's e-mail and leaking the contents; spreading fake news stories to millions of Americans through social media channels; attempting to hack voting systems in at least thirty-nine states; and collaborating with members of the Trump campaign, several of whom pled guilty and went to jail (an investigation is ongoing as of this writing).

That's not all. Third parties gained more than six million votes, many from disaffected Republicans and Democrats. Key Republican leaders, including 2012 nominee Mitt Romney and both Presidents George Bush, skipped their party's convention and publicly came out against Trump, who took office with the lowest approval ratings, and easily the highest disapproval ratings, since that statistic came into use in the 1940s. (At the time, Gallup polls found 63 percent of Americans had a positive view of Obama. On the other hand, 52 percent held a negative view of Clinton, and an all-time high of 61 percent had a negative view of Trump.) Several states, including Wisconsin and North Carolina, passed laws to prevent some of their citizens from voting, impacting the presidential election and other races. There isn't enough room in the pages of this book to analyze all the factors that made 2016 go down the way it did.

Because 2016 was anything but a typical year, it led many Americans to want to learn more about government and elections. All year, on social media and in person, I regularly had strangers ask me all kinds of questions about the process and why certain things were happening. If there's a silver lining to all the craziness of that election (and its even crazier aftermath), it's that it inspired more Americans to get involved, whether that meant the massive protests that followed the inauguration, the fact that many more voters took part in the 2017 off-year elections and 2018 midterms than participated in those same cycles four years earlier, or the founding of groups urging scientists, women, or young people to become candidates for office (voters elected a record 102 women to Congress in 2018). While it is important not to normalize a presidential administration that has routinely attacked US institutions and traditions that both major parties long supported, citizens who paid attention saw some of the system's built-in checks and balances at work.

That said, if there was one line from the first edition of *Votes of Confidence* that showed up most often in reviews of the book, it was: "If there's one thing we know for sure about American government, it's that a lot of Americans don't know much about it."

That remains a real problem.

A September 2017 survey by the Annenberg Public Policy Center at the University of Pennsylvania found that 37 percent of Americans couldn't name any of the rights guaranteed by the

First Amendment to the Constitution, and none of those rights could be identified by a majority. The same poll found only 26 percent could identify the three branches of government—a drop from 36 percent in 2014—and 33 percent could not name a single branch.

In a famous 2011 survey, *Newsweek* magazine figured it would test whether one thousand natural-born US citizens could pass the same citizenship test that immigrants need to take before becoming naturalized. Only 62 percent managed to pass the test. Only 37 percent of the test takers knew how many justices sit on the Supreme Court. Only two-thirds knew when the Declaration of Independence was signed, and 29 percent did not know the identity of the current vice president. (In case you were wondering: nine, 1776 and, at the time, Joe Biden.)

Surveys like these come out pretty often, and they usually lead to news stories about how badly informed voters can be. For example, surveys regularly show that voters think a huge amount of the federal budget goes to foreign aid, when the real number is a teensy fraction of 1 percent. One 2016 poll found the public thought that number was 31 percent (which would be more than Medicare, Social Security, and other major programs), and that 15 percent of people somehow thought more than half the federal budget went to foreign aid. Large percentages of Americans consistently get this wrong and consistently oppose foreign aid because they think it's much more expensive than it has ever been; people believing wrong information influences how they feel about government policy.

That's not even counting the really idiotic examples, like some of the conspiracy theories that flowed freely during the last presidential election. For example, at different points in the campaign, Donald Trump claimed that his opponent's immigration proposals would lead to 600 million or 650 million people moving to the country within a week. That would mean the country doubling its entire population and taking in more people than lived in all of Canada, Central America, and South America combined. To voters who knew that, it was obviously a ridiculous lie; to those who didn't, it might sound like a scary risk. With the spread of misinformation throughout the election cycle, even well-meaning people sometimes wound up believing things that were provably untrue, just because they heard them often enough.

So that's one problem. Another, which we'll talk about later in the book, is that voter turnout in the United States is lower than it is in a lot of other countries, particularly among young voters. In some cases, people think government policy doesn't affect them, so they don't show up. Or they vote in a presidential election, but don't show up for state and local ones. In some states, officials have intentionally tried to make it harder for certain kinds of voters (often minority or young voters) to participate. That means a small percentage of Americans are making decisions about who's in office, and they're often making those decisions based on things they don't really understand. That can't help but cause problems.

At the same time, the country is in the middle of a generational change. Young voters are becoming a larger percentage of the voting-age population, but they also face new challenges when it comes to learning about politics and government. Social media and the shift to online news have made it easy to spread false information (even by accident) and harder to know what's accurate. Schools in some states have cut back on history and civics education, leaving students without the basic level of knowledge they need to become informed voters.

The hope here is that this book can be part of the solution to those problems. In the chapters to come, we'll take a look at how the American system of government came into being and how it's set up. We'll cover primaries and general elections at the national, state, and local levels. We'll look at what you need to do in order to vote, as well as ways you can get more involved. We'll talk about political parties, third parties, debates, campaign financing, ballot initiatives, and more. Along the way, the book includes specific examples from 2016 and earlier campaigns.

Though *Votes of Confidence* was originally published during the 2016 election, the book has been written so that it doesn't apply specifically to any one election—it's about US politics and elections in general. Most of the same information will apply in the 2020 primaries and general election, the 2021 off-year elections, and the 2022 midterms (if those terms aren't familiar, don't worry; we'll talk about those too). In 2020 alone, voters will choose the entire House of Representatives, thirty-three senators, and thirteen governors (in eleven states and two territories). They'll decide whether Democrats or Republicans control both houses of Congress and who controls state legislatures all over the country.

Hopefully, this book will encourage you to think more about American government and politics and to become a more involved citizen, both now and in the many, many elections to come. ∎

CHAPTER 1

AMERICAN GOVERNMENT 101

One of the most important things to remember about the American governmental system is that it's a work in progress. Not just now, but ever since the beginning. In this chapter, we'll look at how and why the system was created and how it's set up.

Two centuries ago, different states had different laws about who was allowed to vote, the majority of Americans had no right to vote at all, state legislatures picked which senators the states sent to Washington . . . and that was still a better system than the country's first try.

More than most other systems of government, ours was designed around the idea of compromise and of checks and balances that prevent any one branch of government from becoming too powerful. That can seem less than ideal if one branch supports a law or policy you like and one of the others is getting in the way. It also means change happens more slowly than in many other countries, because different factions need to get on board to pass a law. On the other hand, that's a good thing when it helps prevent a bad bill from becoming law or stops a president from dismantling a useful program for short-term political reasons.

To be fair, the system definitely has a lot of problems, and we'll get into some of them throughout this book (like why voters in some states have more power than others, or how important fund-raising has become to winning elections). First, though, let's take a quick look at how this uniquely American system came to be.

Section I
How We Got Here: A (Very) Brief History

THE ORIGIN STORY

It's easy to overlook this now, but the original thirteen colonies that became the United States didn't start out with much in common.

Virginia, the oldest colony, was first settled as an economic venture by the struggling London Company—a joint-stock firm whose territory was later taken over by the British crown. The Pilgrims, and later the Puritans, set up separate colonies in modern-day Massachusetts, both wanting to break off from the Anglican Church. (What became Massachusetts was a bit of a frankencolony, stitched together from several parts—including Plymouth, Martha's Vineyard, and Nantucket—that used to be entirely separate colonies.) Rhode Island was founded by Roger Williams, a man kicked out of Plymouth over religious differences (including his being friendly with local American Indians and morally opposing slavery). The youngest of the original thirteen, Georgia, was founded in part as a prison colony for British citizens who couldn't pay their bills. So these future states weren't that united.

The main thing they had in common was that all were colonies of Great Britain (which had not yet formed the United Kingdom), and they all agreed in 1776 to put an end to that arrangement. By the mid-eighteenth century, the future states all had some form of self-government, all at least loosely based on the British parliament. At the same time, the actual parliament back in London didn't give the colonies much say in how they were run, and it passed a series of taxes on the colonies as a way to pay off the debt from the costly Seven Years' War (1756–1763) in North America (also called the French and Indian War). That situation made the idea of "no taxation without representation" a rallying cry in the colonies, as well as a key argument in the Declaration of Independence.

Of course, the colonies teamed up and, with significant assists from France and other countries that saw a chance to weaken Great Britain, won independence in a Revolutionary War that lasted several years (1775–1783). During the war, the alliance of colonies was governed by the Second Continental Congress, a group of representatives from each colony (chosen by each colonial legislature), in which every state had equal say.

The Second Continental Congress—whose members included the first few American presidents, plus big names like Benjamin Franklin, Samuel Adams, and John Hancock—proved it was a good revolutionary organization. It got a lot done at the start of the revolution, from declaring independence to establishing a colonial army under George Washington's command to negotiating alliances with foreign powers. When the war ended, however, it proved it wasn't much more than a good revolutionary organization.

TAKE ONE

The first attempt at an American government, the Articles of Confederation, didn't turn out so well. The articles were rewritten over and over before they were adopted, which watered them down a lot. The Continental Congress finally adopted them in November 1777, and it then took more than three years for the thirteen states to ratify them. The third version of the Continental Congress, renamed the Confederation Congress, or Congress of the Confederation, became the new nation's first federal government—and it was the definition of "small government." It didn't have the power to collect taxes. Or run a standing army. Or regulate trade. Or even mint money.

As you can imagine, with the country still in massive debt from the war, that caused quite a bit of trouble. The federal government asked the states to kick in money but had no authority to actually make them do it. The new nation was in a crippling recession, and inflation was a huge problem. Meanwhile, states argued with one another about their borders, printed their own money, and set their own rules about commerce between states. Many of the best political minds in the country (even Thomas Jefferson, the man most responsible for the Declaration of Independence) chose to serve in state government, where they had more power, rather than in the weak national government.

Here's how weak that government was. A lot of soldiers from the Revolutionary War were still owed payment, or were paid in money that instantly became useless because of inflation, and tried to collect money the federal government didn't have. In 1783, about four hundred Pennsylvania veterans even marched on a congressional meeting in Philadelphia and threatened the

A CAPITAL IDEA

The 1783 uprising in Pennsylvania was part of the inspiration for moving the nation's capital so that it wouldn't be based in any one state, but would sit on federal land and be protected by federal security. With the 1790 Residence Act, Congress established a new home for itself on a diamond-shaped piece of land ceded by Virginia and Maryland.

Only about 68 square miles (176 sq. km), the District of Columbia is home to the key institutions of all three branches of government—the House and Senate, the White House, and the Supreme Court. It's also home to more than half a million citizens who don't live in any state, and there have been several recent attempts to turn the district into one, including statehood legislation introduced to Congress in 2014, 2017, and 2019. Since 2000, with statehood still an issue, District of Columbia residents have been able to choose license plates with the ironic slogan "taxation without representation."

representatives. The state didn't offer to help protect the federal government, which was forced to temporarily flee Pennsylvania. The final straw for many articles supporters was another armed uprising, led by veteran Daniel Shays in Massachusetts in 1786, which featured the state militia fighting against some of the same soldiers who had helped the country win independence.

Obviously, this system wasn't working, and there was a chance the new country would collapse if things didn't change. The proposed solution? A meeting in Philadelphia in the summer of 1787, bringing together some of each state's best minds and tasking them with rewriting the Articles of Confederation.

TAKE TWO

When the men we now think of as the founding fathers got together in Philadelphia, they were supposed to rework the government that already existed. Instead, they decided the Articles of Confederation were such a mess that they were better off just blowing up the whole thing and starting from scratch.

Creating the Constitution took from mid-May to mid-September, with the process including fifty-five delegates chosen to represent twelve states. (Rhode Island didn't want a stronger federal government and stayed away.) There's a famous adage about a camel being a horse designed by committee, and in this case, we're talking about a big committee dealing with a lot of competing goals. Which makes it that much more impressive that they came up with a system that's lasted.

Two of the big conflicts—between big states and small states and between slave states and non-slave states—are perfect examples of how the delegates (or *framers*) had to make some questionable compromises to get the deal done.

One thing to always keep in mind is that, as much as Americans talk about the importance of democracy, the United States isn't technically a democracy. It's a republic. Voters don't vote on most laws; they vote for representatives who vote on the laws. That makes it a system that's democratic in the sense of the people getting to decide who serves in government but without the majority rule of a direct democracy.

Small states weren't keen on too much democracy, because states with more people would be able to overrule states with fewer people. Slave states in the South weren't oblivious to the fact that the northern states had more free people than they did,

THE CONNECTICUT COMPROMISE TODAY

The framers of the Constitution weren't psychic; they didn't know that thirteen states would become fifty, and they couldn't predict just how extreme differences would get between state populations. As of the last census in 2010, California has more than *sixty-six times* as many people as Wyoming . . .

California: 37,253,956
Texas: 25,145,561
New York: 19,378,102

North Dakota: 672,591
Vermont: 625,741
Wyoming: 563,767

. . . but the same number of senators. Which isn't exactly fair to voters in bigger states. As you can guess, though, the states with smaller populations like this arrangement just fine. Changing it would mean a constitutional amendment, which would need either a two-thirds majority in the Senate or a two-thirds majority of state legislatures. The small states will never let that happen. So fair or not, that's the way it is and the way it's going to stay.

----

or that several northern states (five during the 1780s) had already begun to get rid of slavery. Both small states and slave states had the votes to make sure the Constitution wouldn't exist without some kind of compromise.

To make the smaller states happy, the delegates agreed to the Connecticut Compromise, which set up how the Senate and the House of Representatives operate. Having two houses in the legislature wasn't a new idea—the British parliament already had the House of Lords and the House of Commons. The compromise was creating one house in which every state had the same number of votes (the Senate), and one in which states had more or fewer votes based on their populations (the House). Initially, that meant Rhode Island and Delaware would have one representative each, with Virginia's ten representatives the largest delegation. That size disparity between states seems like nothing compared to today's (see sidebar page 19).

Without the Senate, states like Connecticut weren't going to go along with the new government. Without the House, New York and Massachusetts weren't going to be satisfied. And that's a pretty good explanation of politics in the United States in general—getting things done often means finding the solution that the most people can live with, even if nobody's completely happy.

The design of the House as part of that compromise created another issue. The states that already had economies built on slavery weren't willing to give slaves basic human rights, let alone voting rights . . . but they somehow thought it was still okay to count them among their citizens when it came to calculating state populations. Non-slave states didn't like getting a smaller portion of the pie just because they didn't keep several hundred thousand people enslaved. The two sides eventually settled by counting only 60 percent of the slaves as population, treating each slave as only three-fifths of a person. Because of that agreement, slaveholding states would claim 47 seats out of 105 in the first Congress, instead of the 33 they would have had if only free people were counted. This Three-Fifths Compromise, unfortunately, lasted as long as slavery did, and the arguments over the issue were

DON'T SAY NO TO THIS

As a whole generation now knows thanks to Lin-Manuel Miranda, Alexander Hamilton played a key role in the argument for the new Constitution. Starting in October 1787, he teamed up with James Madison and future chief justice John Jay to write *The Federalist Papers*, a series of eighty-five anonymous essays explaining why the current government was inadequate and the ways in which the Constitution would improve things. Most of the essays were originally published in New York newspapers under the pen name "Publius" and spread widely. (The name was clever, but not subtle; Publius Valerius Poplicola was a popular consul who had helped overthrow the last king of Rome and establish the Roman republic.) While all three men wrote as Publius, Hamilton authored fifty-one of the articles, compared to twenty-nine by Madison and only five (due to an illness) by Jay.

....

an uncomfortable preview of how slavery would continue to divide the country until the Civil War settled the issue once and for all.

So the short version of the story is that the delegates emerged from their all-summer meetings with the plan for a new government that was the best they could do, considering thirteen very different states would all have to get on board.

Delaware, in early December 1787, was the first state to ratify the Constitution (and has been bragging about being "the first state" ever since). Considering it was the only state not involved in writing the thing, it makes sense that Rhode Island was the last; it took until 1790, after the first president and Congress had already taken office.

FIXING IT UP

Once it was ratified, the Constitution the framers spent all summer working to write became the law of the land. The framers were smart people, but they weren't perfect, and neither was the system they built. If you look at many of the issues we still face in our politics, you can trace them all the way back to how the system came into existence.

But give the founders some credit—*they knew* the system wasn't perfect, and they set up rules for how to change it. By 1791, the country had already updated the Constitution, adopting the ten amendments known as the Bill of Rights.

Here's the quick version of how it went down. Once the Constitution was drafted, it was submitted to the Confederation Congress, which passed it on to the states for ratification. However, not everyone was on board with the idea. Some still wanted a better version of the Articles of Confederation, not something completely different. Both the pro- and anti-Constitution sides included some famously gifted writers, and they argued in print (often anonymously, see sidebar page 21), trying to get states to accept or reject the Constitution. Nine out of thirteen states had to vote in favor before the new government went into effect.

Obviously, the pro-Constitution side won out in the end, but some of the opposition's points made a lot of sense. One that came up consistently was that the Constitution didn't include language guaranteeing citizens' rights. Considering how important those rights had been in the argument for independence, there was

"I confess that there are several parts of this Constitution which I do not at present approve, but I am not sure I shall never approve them: For having lived long, I have experienced many instances of being obliged by better information, or fuller consideration, to change opinions even on important subjects, which I once thought right, but found to be otherwise."

—BENJAMIN FRANKLIN, IN 1787

definite momentum for the idea of updating the Constitution to spell them out. Three of the biggest states—Massachusetts, Virginia, and New York—agreed to ratify the Constitution only on the condition that such amendments were part of the deal. Still, some Constitution supporters were afraid that amending it so quickly would make the new government look weak and possibly even cause the system to collapse.

James Madison, the future president nicknamed father of the Constitution for his work at the convention, was also one of Virginia's first members of Congress, and he took the controversial step of proposing amendments in the House of Representatives. He originally came up with seventeen, which were approved by the House. The Senate approved another version, cut down to twelve. A committee of representatives from the two bodies then got together and came up with a final draft.

Of the final twelve proposed amendments, ten were ratified on December 15, 1791, and became the Bill of Rights.

GETTING THE VOTE

Some Americans have always had the ability to vote for their representatives—but only some Americans, and it used to be each state's call (not the federal government's). Of the seventeen constitutional amendments after the Bill of Rights, six gave more people the right to vote.

- The Fifteenth Amendment (1870) prohibited the government from denying the vote on "account of race, color, or previous condition of servitude." It took nearly another century to make that idea a reality in some southern states, but it was still a crucial step.
- The Seventeenth Amendment (1913) allowed voters to elect their senators directly, rather than letting state legislatures appoint them. Senators then had to actually campaign and appeal to the public, giving voters more say.
- The Nineteenth Amendment (1920) established that women had the right to vote, saying governments could not deny that right "on account of sex." A few western states already had

....

The First Amendment packs a lot into just one sentence. It guarantees that the government will not establish religion—meaning not only that the United States wasn't founded as a Christian nation, but that it was specifically founded as a non-Christian nation (and not a nation of any other religion). It guarantees free speech and a free press, freedom to practice any religion, freedom to assemble, and freedom to petition the

equal voting rights for women starting in the late nineteenth century, but this guaranteed them nationwide.

- The Twenty-Third Amendment (1961) gave citizens of the District of Columbia the right to vote in presidential elections, with the district casting the same number of electoral votes as the smallest states.
- The Twenty-Fourth Amendment (1964) made it illegal to use poll taxes or similar taxes to prevent voting in federal elections. Several southern states had used these taxes as a way to discriminate against African American voters—a way to get around the Thirteenth Amendment—and deny their equal voting rights.
- The Twenty-Sixth Amendment (1971) lowered the voting age from twenty-one to eighteen nationwide. Here, too, some states already had lower voting ages, but this set the same age in every state. It was partly a reaction to eighteen-year-old citizens being drafted into the military during the conflict in Vietnam without getting any say in who was drafting them.

....

government. Other amendments prevent the government from forcing citizens to house soldiers, give citizens the right to a "speedy and public" trial by jury, and prevent excessive punishment. (Fun fact: One of the original amendments that didn't make the cut in 1791 was ratified later. Much later, in 1992, as the Twenty-Seventh Amendment. The most recent amendment, it prevents the current Congress from giving itself a pay raise; any raise needs to go into effect after the next congressional election, once voters get a chance to replace some members of Congress.)

Because the amendments are all pretty short in terms of wording, there's always been disagreement about exactly how far some of their protections go. For years, people have argued about what the Second Amendment meant by "a well-regulated militia" when it comes to the right to own weapons, or what the Eighth Amendment meant by "cruel and unusual punishments" when it comes to outlawing those punishments.

The Ninth and Tenth Amendments are often underrated, but they played big roles in how American government took shape. The Ninth explains that just because a right isn't specifically spelled out in the Constitution, that doesn't mean citizens don't have that right. The Tenth establishes the idea of federalism—the division of power between the federal government and state governments. It says that powers not given to the federal government by the Constitution are given to the states or to the people.

Only seventeen other amendments have been ratified since the Bill of Rights, proving that the Constitution is difficult to change, but that it can be done. Many of those later amendments had to do with expanding voting rights (see sidebar page 24). Others ended slavery (the Thirteenth, ratified in 1865), established a federal income tax (the Sixteenth, ratified in 1913), or clarified the process for when and how the vice president becomes president (the Twenty-Fifth, ratified in 1967). Famously, the Eighteenth Amendment banned the manufacture and sale of alcohol in the United States, creating Prohibition when it was ratified in 1919, only to have the Twenty-First Amendment completely repeal it in 1933.

So that's a (very) short version of how the American government became the system we know and how it has the concepts of compromise and an evolving role for government baked into the cake. Now we'll take a similarly quick look at how that system's set up and who does what.

Section II
Branching Out: How the System Works

Just as it balanced the needs of different states, the Constitution also balanced the power of different parts of the government. Great Britain had gone through some rather bloody struggles between kings and parliaments, and the framers figured it was a good idea to avoid similar experiences.

One big innovation was setting up a government with three branches—executive, legislative, and judicial—and dividing their powers. What the framers did here was take existing ideas from a bunch of other governments and rearrange them in a different way, making a new recipe out of familiar ingredients.

The result is a bit like a much more complex game of rock-paper-scissors, where every branch has some power to defeat something another wants to do. Depending on how in sync the different branches are, the separation of powers can cause total gridlock, or it can produce laws (and enforcement of those laws) that combine the best ideas from the different branches. A lot of times, the results land somewhere in the middle.

A key part of understanding government is understanding who does what. It gets a lot more complicated than what can fit in this chapter, but there are some main differences between the branches and some key roles that are important for citizens to understand. Election-year news coverage tends to focus on the presidential race—after all, it's the one race in which every American voter can cast a ballot—but the federal government goes far beyond the presidency.

LEGISLATIVE BRANCH

Congress, the legislative branch, is the one that would look most familiar to people from the original colonies, as it was a modified version of the British parliament they already knew.

Thanks to the Connecticut Compromise (page 19), the American legislature is made up of two houses: the two-members-per-state Senate and the based-on-population House of Representatives. The size of the Senate grows by two every time a new state joins the Union. So with fifty states, there are one hundred senators. That part's simple.

As for the House, its members used to be in charge of deciding how many colleagues they had. From just 65 members in 1789, the House grew to more than 200 in 1821, and the number passed 300 in 1883. Eventually, in 1911, Congress passed a law limiting House membership to 435 members. There used to be some exceptions to that rule, and Congress later passed more laws to set up how that membership limit would be enforced.

The short version is that every ten years, based on the results of the national census, seats are shifted around by population. Every state still gets at least one representative, but the rest are divvied up based on the census results. So a state gaining people (or gaining fewer people than other states, or actually losing population) has a real impact on how much say that state has in Congress. When new states joined, their representation was included in the 435 seats, so other states needed to lose seats in the process. It's also worth pointing out that American citizens in Washington, DC, as well as in Puerto Rico and other overseas territories, can only elect nonvoting representatives (who can speak about issues during congressional debates). They don't count among the 435, because the others don't count their votes; so far, not enough people have seen the irony for this to change.

As for what those one hundred senators and 435 representatives do, Congress has what's arguably the most important job in the federal government—passing laws. Bills have to pass both the House and the Senate to become laws, and the process of getting that done can be complicated.

PASSING THE LAWS

The first step is a member of Congress introducing a bill. That senator or representative (or their staff) might have written the bill, or it could have been written by anyone else and introduced by the representative. Examples can range from the cute (schoolchildren submitting a bill to name their state bird), to the practical (the president's team writing the first draft of a bill he or she promised to introduce during the election), to the unsavory but common (a lobbyist for an industry writing a bill that benefits that industry). The concept is that, in theory, any American can help create a law, as long as they can get their representative to back the idea.

Both houses then have to pass their own versions of a bill. In each body, members are assigned to specific committees, and each committee branches off into several smaller subcommittees. Whichever political party has control of the chamber (by holding more seats) also decides who's in charge of each committee, but any committee or subcommittee will include both Democrats and Republicans.

When a bill is introduced, it goes to a subcommittee to be reviewed and edited. If the majority of a subcommittee can agree on a version, then it goes to the full committee, which also gets to make changes. Only after a bill passes the full committee does it go to the whole House or the whole Senate for a floor vote. The vast majority of the thousands of bills introduced every year never even get past the committee stage. For those that do, a floor vote has to be scheduled by the House or Senate leadership, and one way to kill a bill the leadership doesn't like is to delay scheduling it or just never schedule it at all.

If a bill somehow survives that whole obstacle course and is passed by either the House or the Senate, it must also pass the other chamber, which makes its own changes. Then the two passed versions need to be merged into one final bill, and a committee of senators and representatives works together to produce the final, final version (a process often called *reconciliation*). That version, based on the enormous game of telephone it takes to produce it, can look a lot different from the version originally introduced. Then both houses vote again to approve it. Only after all that does the bill go to the president for a signature.

WHAT'S DIFFERENT

Besides the membership numbers, the Constitution established a few other differences between the House and the Senate. All bills to raise revenue (including taxes) need to start in the House. This was another one of those ideas the framers took from the home country, because all revenue bills in British parliament had to originate in the House of Commons, the house that represented more of the population. Spending bills also originate in the House, but that's more of a tradition that developed and is now pretty much set in stone.

The Senate gets a few extra powers the House doesn't have. When the president makes appointments, those choices must be confirmed by a majority of the Senate. That's a big deal; it affects who becomes ambassadors, cabinet officials, federal judges, you name it. (The one exception is when the vice president dies or resigns while in office. In that case, both the House and Senate need to confirm the replacement.) Any treaty the president makes with another country also needs the support of two-thirds of the Senate. (International trade deals need both House and Senate approval.)

When federal officials are impeached for allegedly committing a crime, the House brings the charges and the Senate tries them. If two-thirds of the Senate votes to convict, the official is removed from office. Impeachment is rare; the House has only voted to impeach nineteen officials throughout history. (Two presidents have been impeached by the House but stayed in office because they were acquitted by the Senate—Andrew Johnson in 1868 and Bill Clinton in 1998 [see sidebar on page 32]. Same thing with the only impeached Supreme Court justice, Samuel Chase, in 1804.) Still, it's always there as a threat if an official commits serious crimes (and Congress chooses to hold them accountable); several officials have resigned before facing impeachment.

UNDERSTANDING IMPEACHMENT

Because impeachment is rare, it is also often misunderstood.

For one thing, just because someone is impeached doesn't mean he or she is guilty; it means that enough members of the House consider the case worth pursuing. It's like any criminal or civil case—going to court isn't the same thing as getting convicted.

As the examples of Andrew Johnson and Bill Clinton prove, impeached officials can beat the rap and stay in office. The charges against Johnson focused primarily on his decision to replace Secretary of War Edwin Stanton with former general (and future president) Ulysses S. Grant. Those against Clinton mostly focused on his sexual relationship with a White House intern, which he had denied under oath. In Johnson's case, the Senate voted 35–19 against him, but 36 votes were needed to convict. In Clinton's case, the Senate clearly sided with him, voting 55–45 to acquit.

Ask many Americans about impeached presidents, and they'll think of Richard Nixon—but he was never actually impeached. In 1974 Nixon became the first (and, as of this writing, only) president to resign from office, as a result of the Watergate scandal. The scandal began with a break-in at the Democratic National Committee's headquarters (in Washington's Watergate Hotel), which

....

Otherwise, many of the differences between the houses are less about what they do and more about how they do it.

Partly because the House has so many members, any speech a representative gives on the floor must be about the bill under discussion, and there are time limits on those speeches. While

The impeachment process didn't kick Andrew Johnson out of office, but it came awfully close.

Nixon and other White House officials tried to cover up. Investigations into the break-in—by the *Washington Post* and the FBI—uncovered other illegal White House activities, including wiretapping and harassing of Nixon's political opponents. The House was preparing to impeach Nixon, but he resigned before the process was complete.

House members can add amendments to a bill during a floor debate, the chamber's rules really limit when and how they can do that.

In the Senate, that's another story. Members can add amendments at any point during the discussion on a bill. Amendments

KILLING TIME

There can be something romantic about the filibuster, like the famous scene in the movie *Mr. Smith Goes to Washington*, in which Jimmy Stewart's character, exhausted and frustrated, keeps speaking to defend himself against trumped-up charges made by a corrupt colleague and exposes the villain's real motives to the whole country.

Historically, filibusters used to look a bit like that, even when the motives were far less admirable. Segregationist senator Strom Thurmond set a record when he notoriously filibustered the Civil Rights Act of 1957 by talking for more than twenty-four hours, including reading every state's election laws in alphabetical order. (Thankfully, his protest failed, and that bill became a law.)

Lately, that kind of hold-the-floor filibuster doesn't happen much (and when it does, it's usually a political-theater move). Instead, if the minority party knows that the majority can't get the sixty votes needed to stop a filibuster, it can usually just filibuster a motion to proceed—which keeps the bill or nominee from being debated at all.

It's also fair to say the filibuster has been abused. Even though the first one took place in 1837 (and the rules that allow it go back three decades earlier), it has been used far more often since 1990 than in the rest of American history combined. Because bills otherwise

don't need to have much to do with the bill either. (These late-in-the-game amendments are often called *riders*.) Senators have been known to introduce amendments that seem totally irrelevant, either as a way to get their pet issue attached to a more popular bill or as a way to kill a whole bill by adding a toxic amendment nobody

The pure motives (and pure energy) of Jefferson Smith, played by Jimmy Stewart in *Mr. Smith Goes to Washington*, made his fictional filibuster one to remember.

pass with fifty-one out of one hundred votes, and a Senate-passed procedural rule is the reason sixty out of one hundred are now often needed, it's no wonder the filibuster is heavily criticized.

The Republican-controlled 111th Congress (2009–2011) filibustered so many presidential nominees that it led to serious filibuster reform. In 2013 the majority of senators voted to prevent the use of the filibuster for executive branch and judicial nominees, other than for the Supreme Court—and the Senate removed that Supreme Court exception in 2017. (A majority of the Senate still needs to confirm the appointments.) Bills, however, can still be filibustered as always.

. . . .

wants to support. The big annual spending bills that provide the budget for whole government departments often get hit with riders, because if members can get an amendment through, the other senators probably won't vote down the whole bill and start from scratch just to defeat an amendment. Senators can add, remove,

SPEAKER NOTES

Once the Speaker is in power, it's usually up to the rest of the party caucus in the House to replace them. If the party loses power, other members will often organize a challenge to the Speaker, and an intra-party House vote will decide whether he or she is replaced. That's the case for all the leadership positions in the House and Senate.

Sometimes, the same people stay in leadership even when the party loses power. The most experienced Speaker in history, Sam Rayburn (D-Texas) had the gig for more than seventeen years between 1940 and 1961. Even though the Republicans won House control twice in that span, costing him the speakership, his party kept Rayburn as its leader in the chamber. Because control of the House went back and forth, he served a record three stints as Speaker, tying him with Henry Clay (Whig-Kentucky), who faced a similar situation between 1811 and 1825.

In 2007 Nancy Pelosi (D-California) became the first female Speaker of the House, making her the highest-ranking woman in the

or set aside (*table*) amendments until the amendment period ends. Then the bill is read as is, and the Senate votes on it.

Senate rules also allow senators to speak for as long as they want about any issue, until they give up their time. Known as the *filibuster* (see sidebar on page 34), this tactic means any senator can delay a vote on a bill or on a nominee awaiting con-firmation, until sixty other senators vote to stop them (a process called *cloture*).

Keep in mind that these Senate rules don't come from the

history of the federal government to that point. Even after Republicans regained control of the House in the 2010 election, she remained the Democratic leader in the House and became Speaker again after the Democrats gained forty seats in the 2018 midterm elections.

Other times, speakers resign if they know a challenge is coming. In 1998 House Republicans lost seats in a midterm just four years after taking power, which was a historic loss for an opposition party. (Usually the president's party loses seats in a midterm.) Even though Republicans still held a House majority (just a much smaller one), Newt Gingrich (R-Georgia) resigned as Speaker and announced he was also retiring from his House seat.

Of course, voters have one way to replace Speakers of the House—not reelecting them to their own House seat. It happened most recently to Tom Foley (D-Washington) in 1994, and before that to Galusha Grow (R-Pennsylvania) back in 1862. Eric Cantor (R-Virginia), the House majority leader, lost his own seat in a primary in 2014.

....

Constitution, and in some cases, they aren't even laws; they're rules the Senate passed over time that have become tradition.

LEADERSHIP

The leadership of the House and Senate is decided by which political party has the most seats. In the Senate, the party with more seats elects a majority leader and a majority whip (the number two job includes enforcing party discipline, hence the name). The party with the second most seats will elect a minority leader and minority whip. All these roles can be filled by any senator. Independent or third-party senators not affiliated with either major party will organize, or *caucus*, with one or the other and vote for that party's leadership. (Since 2000, there have been six independents in the Senate, but never more than three at a time.)

Being a senator is usually considered a better job than being a member of the House, and senators are much more likely to be considered serious contenders for president. For one thing, they have already appealed to voters across a full state instead of just a district, which means they have a wider political base than most House members and more experience talking to voters.

However, one of the most desirable jobs in government is the Speaker of the House. Voters don't get to pick the Speaker; he or she is chosen by the party that controls more seats in the House (much like how prime ministers are selected in other countries). The Speaker presides over the House, so he or she gets to call on members who want to speak, decide which bills in the queue get discussed in which order, pick which bills go to committee, and choose which members serve on any special committee in the House. It's arguably the most important job in government other than the president—and, after the vice president, the next in the line of presidential succession—but only voters in the person's home district get to vote on whether that candidate is elected to Congress, and only other members of Congress get to decide whether that representative becomes the Speaker. The Speaker's party also has a majority leader and a majority whip, and the House has a leader and a whip for the minority party.

As powerful as the Speaker is—and the other House and Senate leaders are no weaklings either—the most powerful job is in the executive branch.

EXECUTIVE BRANCH

The office of president is something we now take for granted, but it was a totally new concept in 1787. Plenty of countries at the time had one powerful figure in charge, but that usually meant a king or queen who got the job by being born to the right parents or a dictator who took over by force.

The framers agreed that the country shouldn't have a king. (Some Americans had suggested one right after the revolution, but George Washington—the most obvious candidate—turned down the offer.) And obviously, most people weren't into the idea of the states going through all the work of becoming independent just to hand over power to any one person. Still, one of the many problems with the Articles of Confederation was that the country had no clear leader.

With the government taking on more responsibility under the new Constitution, it became more important to have someone in the top job who would carry out the country's laws. The name *president* comes from "preside," and was a term already used for the heads of some organizations, but the United States became the first country to call its leader by that title. (Now lots of countries have presidents, though it isn't always their highest office.)

The president is always the most recognizable part of the American government, and he or she is the one person every voter can vote for (or against). The president has a lot of powers, but remember, he or she doesn't make laws. The president can, and usually does, suggest a long list of ideas to turn into laws, but Congress must actually pass them.

Instead, the president has a few major ways to influence policy. First, any bill passed by Congress goes to the president for a signature, and the president's autograph makes it a law. The president also has the authority to veto (or block) anything Congress passes, either by sending the bill back unsigned or by leaving it unsigned when Congress adjourns.

The first option means Congress has a chance to override the veto, but only if two-thirds of both the House and Senate agree—in theory, this was a way to make sure the president can't just overrule bills that have overwhelming support. (Of more than 2,500 vetoes, only 111 have ever been overturned as of June 2019.) The second option, called a pocket veto, can't be overridden, because Congress isn't in session to do so. Franklin Roosevelt used the veto more than any other president (635 times), followed by Grover Cleveland (414 times). Seven presidents never used it at all—a list that includes a few who weren't in office long, but also John Adams and Thomas Jefferson. Usually, the threat of a veto is a way for presidents to get Congress to take their suggestions seriously, since there's not much point in spending a lot of time and effort writing and passing a law that's just going to be vetoed.

In theory, every federal law is supposed to be passed by Congress, and most are. In reality, over time, the president has gained the authority to handle certain things without Congress's approval. A lot of how the executive branch now operates is that way because of how George Washington chose to do it. Because there was no real blueprint for what a president does, he became the blueprint.

One example is the executive order, which means the president single-handedly creates a rule for the government to follow.

The president's political opponents often complain about executive orders, because the president is essentially making a law without Congress, but it's less common than it used to be. The last five full-term presidents (Barack Obama, Bill Clinton, the two George Bushes, and Ronald Reagan) combined to issue fewer executive orders than Calvin Coolidge did by himself—1,152 compared to 1,203—and Coolidge is only number three on the all-time list.

Foreign policy is an area where the president has quite a bit of authority. As the public face of the country, he or she meets with other world leaders and can negotiate treaties and other agreements. Treaties still need Senate approval, but fewer than one in ten international agreements is an actual treaty. The president is also commander in chief of the armed forces and tends to receive a lot of leeway when it comes to using them. According to the Constitution, only Congress can declare war, but in practice, the president often takes military action without that declaration. The United States hasn't fought a declared war since World War II, though that didn't make the numerous conflicts since 1945 (from Korea to Vietnam to Afghanistan to Iraq) any less deadly or expensive.

The president also takes the lead in filling a lot of federal jobs—just between getting elected in November and taking office in January, the president is responsible for literally thousands of federal appointments. Appointing federal officials and judges is a huge responsibility, and a lot of things for which the president will be able to take credit (or blame) have to do with who runs various federal departments. As mentioned earlier, presidential appointments must be confirmed by a majority of the Senate as part of the system's checks and balances. As the country has grown and the government has grown with it, there are more executive branch departments and more responsibilities housed within them.

THE REST OF THE BRANCH

The executive branch isn't just the office of the president.

Of course, there's the vice president, whose job is not well defined. The Constitution names the veep "president of the Senate," which means casting the deciding vote if the Senate is stuck in a 50–50 tie. This has happened fewer than 250 times and was much more common in the country's early years. The vice president is also first in line to take over if the president dies, resigns, or is otherwise unable to do the job. That is legitimately important— the vice president has needed to take over nine times, starting with John Tyler subbing in for William Henry Harrison in 1841, when the president died from illness just a month into his term.

For a long time, the vice president didn't have much of an active role in government at all, other than being the party's most likely nominee for the next election. Not that long ago, it wasn't unusual for the president and vice president to barely interact, because the choice of the number two was more about winning the election and less about running the country. That's gradually changed in the last few decades, as presidents began to select their own running mates and to pick someone they could rely on as an adviser or involve in specific tasks. Al Gore, Dick Cheney, and Joe Biden were particularly active, and they were presented during the elections as experienced leaders who would be key parts of the administration.

There's also the president's cabinet, which oversees quite a few federal departments and has grown significantly since the early days. George Washington had exactly four cabinet members: Secretary of State Thomas Jefferson, Secretary of the Treasury Alexander Hamilton, Secretary of War Henry Knox, and Attorney General Edmund Randolph. At this point, there are fifteen cabinet departments, including the Department of Energy, the Department of Veterans Affairs, and the Department of Transportation. The newest cabinet-level department, the Department of Homeland Security, was created in 2002 by, for better or worse, combining twenty-two existing federal agencies into one. And those are just a few examples (see sidebar on page 45).

The executive branch is in charge of enforcing the laws day to day. For example, if Congress passes a bill making something a federal crime, the Department of Justice (headed by the attorney general) handles the prosecution of those crimes. Or if Congress passes a bill funding an environmental cleanup program, the Environmental Protection Agency decides how and where the funds will be used. Each cabinet department has the authority to make rules governing its areas of expertise, and the departments also determine how to prioritize their activities. As long as there isn't unlimited money or unlimited staffers, cabinet departments will always have to make tough calls about how to spend their budgets and about where their employees should devote their time.

In addition, the power of cabinet departments goes well beyond just enforcing existing laws. At this point, there are hundreds of federal agencies with specific jobs, and most are housed within one cabinet department or another. For example, the Federal Emergency Management Agency (FEMA), which handles the federal government's response to natural disasters such as hurricanes and tornadoes, is part of the Department of Homeland Security (DHS), includes thousands of employees, and has a budget of several billion dollars. The United States Secret Service, which provides agents who protect the president and other federal officials, is also part of DHS. So is the Transportation Security Administration (TSA), which handles security at all United States airports. So is the United States Coast Guard. So are a lot of other huge agencies with major roles in how the country operates.

Examples like that exist for every cabinet department. Much of the executive branch's power at this point has little to do directly with the president and more to do with the thousands and thousands of workers spread out across the federal bureaucracy.

The executive branch also includes the Executive Office of the President, which includes the chief of staff, the team that the president works with daily (most of the main characters on the TV show *The West Wing* are part of the EOP), and a number of advisers who keep the president up to date on specific aspects of the country.

Other than picking the president and vice president, voters don't have much say in who fills all these important jobs. An often-overlooked part of evaluating presidential candidates is getting a sense of the kinds of officials they'll appoint to fill these positions. The same thing applies when it comes to the members of the third branch of government.

CABINET CONTENTS

Since the days of George Washington's four-man cabinet, the cabinet has gotten a lot fuller. Plus, the vice president is now part of it. And there are seven other officials with cabinet-level rank, even though they don't lead cabinet departments. When the president calls a cabinet meeting, it can involve all of the following people:

- Vice President
- Secretary of State
- Secretary of the Treasury
- Secretary of Defense
- Attorney General
- Secretary of the Interior
- Secretary of Agriculture
- Secretary of Commerce
- Secretary of Labor
- Secretary of Health and Human Services
- Secretary of Housing and Urban Development
- Secretary of Transportation
- Secretary of Energy
- Secretary of Education
- Secretary of Veterans Affairs
- Secretary of Homeland Security
- White House Chief of Staff
- Administrator of the Environmental Protection Agency
- Director of the Office of Management and Budget
- United States Trade Representative
- Ambassador to the United Nations
- Chair of the Council of Economic Advisers
- Administrator of the Small Business Administration

Starting in the 1980s, in a fit of Cold War paranoia, a tradition began in which, during the State of the Union address or other times when the whole government meets in one place, one member of the cabinet always stays far away. This "designated survivor" practice makes sure somebody in the line of presidential succession is still around to take over in case of a nuclear strike, massive attack, natural disaster, or any other unlikely action-movie scenario.

JUDICIAL BRANCH

The entire Constitution is only forty-four hundred words long (this chapter alone is more than twice that long), so it leaves a lot of things open to interpretation. That's where the third branch, the judiciary, gets involved. The judges the president appoints will often stay in office far longer than he or she does.

Even after Congress and the president have worked out their differences and passed a law, that doesn't automatically mean that the law is constitutional. If the courts find a law unconstitutional, they can completely overrule it, making the judicial branch an important part of the checks-and-balances concept.

While the Constitution gives federal judges significant power, including the ability to keep their job for as long as they want it (unless they do something problematic enough to get them impeached), it doesn't say anything at all about their qualifications. There are age requirements for the president and vice president (at least thirty-five), senators (thirty and up), and congressmen (twenty-five and up), but not for judges. The Constitution doesn't even require judges to be lawyers or have law degrees—though it's usually a sure thing that anyone appointed to the federal bench will have a law background.

The Supreme Court is, as the name suggests, the top court and the one with final say. The nine justices serve for life or until they decide to retire, and the odd number makes sure they don't wind up tied on important issues. That wasn't always true—the first Supreme Court had just six justices, making the chief justice the tiebreaker. The number of justices changed a few times, but it's been set at nine since 1837.

Supreme Court justices are appointed by the president, but

like cabinet secretaries and other appointees, they must also be confirmed by a majority of the Senate. They can last a long time on the bench. The longest-serving Supreme Court justice, William O. Douglas, was appointed by Franklin Roosevelt in 1939 and didn't retire until 1975 (a thirty-six-year span that included seven presidents). All but four presidents have nominated at least one justice. While some justices take the "lifetime" appointment seriously and die while a member of the court, more than fifty others retired, usually (but not always) timing it so presidents of their own political parties were able to pick their replacements.

Of the thousands of cases the Supreme Court is asked to hear every year, it chooses to hear fewer than one hundred on average. Most cases the Supreme Court hears are appeals of lower court decisions—either cases from federal circuit courts or cases that have worked up to a state supreme court and are then taken to the federal level. (The Supreme Court is also the first stop for cases in which one state sues another state, though that doesn't happen much anymore.)

If the Supreme Court decides not to hear a case, the lower court's decision stands. Keep in mind that the judges on other federal courts are also presidential appointees, also go through confirmation, and also serve as long as they want while they're in good standing.

DIFFERENT LEVELS

When people talk about "the government," they usually mean the federal government. That makes sense; it has the highest profile and has an impact on the largest number of citizens.

SUPREME DECISIONS

When people talk about "government" or "Washington," they often overlook the role of the federal court system, which has played no small role in creating the country we have today. Here are just a few examples of Supreme Court decisions that made the country more democratic by giving citizens more rights or better defining the ones they already have:

- *Brown v. The Board of Education of Topeka* in 1954: Ruled that racial segregation was unconstitutional and that "separate but equal" was by definition not equal. This case forced the president to help integrate schools in the South and was an early victory for the civil rights movement.
- *Gideon v. Wainwright* in 1963: Ruled that the Sixth Amendment guarantees that anyone charged with a crime is entitled to a lawyer, even if they can't afford one.
- *Reynolds v. Sims* in 1964: Ruled that states had to design their congressional districts so that they had roughly equal populations. The case got rid of Alabama's system, which divided the districts by county, no matter how many people lived in each one.

In your day-to-day life, though, odds are that your state and local governments have even more of a direct impact on you (or at least just as big of one).

Need a few examples? The speed limit for drivers is different from state to state. So is the amount of the fine you'll get

- *Griswold v. Connecticut* in 1965: Established that Americans have a right to privacy under the First Amendment. Like any right, there are situations in which privacy isn't absolute, but this ruling at least guaranteed that it's a constitutional right.
- *Miranda v. Arizona* in 1966: Ruled that police must inform arrested suspects of their constitutional rights. The well-known wording "You have the right to remain silent. Anything you say can and will be used against you . . ." was created in response to this ruling, and the listed rights are called *Miranda rights*.
- *Loving v. Virginia* in 1967: Ruled that state laws banning interracial marriage are unconstitutional.
- *Roe v. Wade* in 1973: Established that women have the right to have an abortion. This ruling turned abortion into a major campaign issue for decades.
- *Reno v. ACLU* in 1997: Ruled that the First Amendment right to free speech applies to the Internet. As the internet was then new technology for most Americans, this was a big decision.
- *Obergefell v. Hodges* in 2015: Ruled that same-sex marriage is a constitutional right and that state and federal laws against it are unconstitutional.

if you're pulled over for speeding. Public elementary schools and high schools are funded differently depending on the state and the local level—some get their money from local property taxes or from the state government. Property taxes for homeowners are set by state or local governments, not the federal one.

DANGEROUS PRECEDENT

In 2016 Congress set a precedent that will haunt American politics for decades to come. Supreme Court justice Antonin Scalia, one of the court's most conservative voices, died in his sleep while on a February hunting trip. One month later, President Barack Obama nominated Merrick Garland to replace Scalia on the bench, choosing a centrist judge who had previously received praise from both Democrats and Republicans. (Republican senator Orrin Hatch had even suggested Garland as a "consensus nominee" when a seat opened in 2010.)

However, Republican leaders in the Senate announced that they would not hold hearings for Garland—or any other Obama nominee—and would wait until the next president took office in 2017. Senate majority leader Mitch McConnell (R-Kentucky) claimed a president shouldn't nominate a justice during a presidential election year, a transparently partisan excuse, considering Grover Cleveland and Ronald Reagan each had a Supreme Court nominee confirmed in that same situation (and the president is still supposed to do his or her job, including making appointments, during an election year). While individual nominees have been rejected on their own merits in the past, this was a problematic case because the objection was not with Garland but with the president's previously unchallenged right (and responsibility) to nominate a justice.

The Senate never held a hearing for Garland, waiting to fill the seat until Donald Trump nominated Neil Gorsuch in January 2017. In other words, McConnell and his allies held a Supreme Court seat hostage until their party took over the White House. Now that they've gotten away with it, it will be difficult to stop either party from pulling that kind of thing again and again.

If you rent a place, how much your landlord pays in property taxes probably plays a role in how much he or she charges you.

On other issues, both the federal and state governments can have a say, but the federal government has the final one. If you've ever worked a minimum-wage job, that's a good example, because "minimum wage" means something completely different depending on where you live. Between 2007 and 2010, the federal minimum wage went up from $5.15 an hour to $7.25 an hour (an extra $84 a week for a full-time job) and, as of this writing, it's still $7.25 (if it had increased just enough to match inflation since 2010, it would be $8.25 instead). Two states have state minimum wages below that number, but the federal law overrules them, so workers still make $7.25. Six other states don't have a state minimum wage, so the federal law automatically sets the minimum. Meanwhile, by 2015, California had a $9 per hour minimum, which went up to $10 in 2016 and increases annually, to $15 by 2022. Several other states, including Arizona, Colorado, and Oregon, are also in the midst of annual increases, thanks to ballot measures voters passed in 2016 (more on those later). Some cities have minimum wages even higher than that. San Francisco and Seattle, for example, set it at $15 per hour, more than twice the federal minimum.

Or take taxes, if you want a more complicated example. If you have a job or other revenue source, and you make above a certain level of income, you need to pay federal income tax plus federal payroll taxes (which pay for Social Security and Medicare). Whether you also pay state taxes, though, depends on where you live. In Texas, there's no state income tax. Same with Florida. Or

Alaska, Nevada, or Washington State. On the other hand, as of 2015, California has a state tax that ranges from about 1 percent to more than 12 percent, though you need to make a lot of money before the bigger number applies to you.

Some cities even have their own income tax. So if you live in New York City, you pay a city tax (about 3 percent), plus the state tax, plus the federal income tax and payroll tax. Someone making the same money in Miami is only paying federal income tax. Just like income tax is different from state to state, so is sales tax. Some states have it, and some don't. Some cities or counties have their own sales tax, whether or not there's also a state sales tax.

In other words, the state (and local) governments still get to make their own rules, as long as they don't break national rules. This definitely applies to voting, which we'll cover more in later chapters.

Just as the founders divided the role of government between the different branches, they also divided the roles between the government in Washington and the governments of the different states. This is federalism in action, and the legal basis for it comes from the Tenth Amendment to the Constitution, which says powers not outlined in the Constitution usually belong to the states. When the United States formed from separate states with separate governments, federalism let them keep some of their differences while becoming one country.

HOW THEY WORK

Individual state governments all have their own branches, and they look a lot like the branches of the federal government.

The governor heads up the state's executive branch, and states have various departments that work like state-level cabinet departments. They're different in every state, but most states have an office that deals with education or agriculture or transportation. (Not all federal departments have a state equivalent; states don't exactly need their own Departments of Defense.)

Just as the federal executive branch has a range of cabinet offices, states can have similar executive positions. It's hard to generalize, because the fifty states have fifty different setups, but there are a few offices worth pointing out.

Every state has its own attorney general, who is the state's top legal officer in the same way the US attorney general fills that role for the country. All but three states have a secretary of state (a few call theirs the secretary of the commonwealth). Depending on the state, that job can be one of the most powerful offices, or it can be a mostly administrative job dealing with things like voter registration and drivers' licenses. Every state except Texas has a treasurer, who is in charge of managing the state's money. Forty-five states have a lieutenant governor, and the states have different ways of picking them (see sidebar on page 54). They can be paired up with the governor on a ticket, like the president and vice president, or they can be elected separately. In that case, they can even represent different political parties.

Depending on the state, jobs such as attorney general or secretary of state can be filled by voters in a general election, by an appointment from the governor, or by an election in the state legislature. Your state might have other statewide offices as well. The more of those officials that voters (rather than other officials) get

STRANGE BEDFELLOWS

The lieutenant governor's job is a good example of how different state governments can be. In Texas, the lieutenant governor arguably has more power than the governor. In Wyoming, the job doesn't exist. Then there's Illinois, where weird things happen.

In Illinois, for ages the governor and lieutenant governor ran in separate primaries, then as one ticket in the general election. Candidates for governor could tell voters who they wanted in the LG spot, but they didn't always do that. (And when they did, voters didn't need to listen.)

Back in 1986, Mark Fairchild, a candidate from conspiracy theorist Lyndon LaRouche's party, ran in the Democratic primary for lieutenant governor and won an upset victory against the actual Democrats. Fairchild was then paired up for the general election with Democrat Adlai Stevenson III, who had no legal way to drop him from the ticket. Stevenson, who had been expected to win in

....

to select, the more say voters have in how the state runs, and the less likely it is that one political party dominates the state.

Like their Washington equivalent, nearly all state legislatures include both a state House of Representatives and a state senate. Three states originally had a one-body legislature but switched from unicameral to bicameral. (Nebraska went the opposite direction, becoming the only state with a unicameral legislature in the 1930s. It has a Senate but no House, and has stuck with that arrangement ever since.)

Each state has its own court system to handle any violations of state law that don't have federal implications—in other words,

November, chose to give up his party's gubernatorial nomination and run on a third-party ticket, and lost to the Republican nominee. In 2002 Rod Blagojevich won a close three-way race for the Democratic gubernatorial nomination, while Pat Quinn easily won the nod for the number two job. They had little in common and little to do with each other after the election. In 2008 Blagojevich was arrested after being caught on tape trying to sell political appointments, so the state legislature impeached him and removed him from office. Blagojevich went to prison (an unfortunate tradition among Illinois governors), while Quinn—a longtime good-government activist before becoming a politician and Blagojevich's opposite on ethics issues— became the new governor. During Quinn's administration, the state put an end to this odd practice; since 2014, would-be governors choose their own lieutenants after winning their party's nomination.

....

most court cases. For example, federal courts rarely need to get involved with a couple getting divorced or a thief on trial for the crime. If you get a speeding ticket, nobody's going to make a federal case out of it—you'll pay a fine to the state or county or go to a state or county court if you want to fight it.

The judicial branch at the federal level is all appointed. But in one of the quirks of American government that often baffles people living in other democratic countries, some states allow voters to choose their own judges. Some let you vote to keep or remove the judges already there, and others allow judges to campaign just like any other elected official. (The reason many find that weird is that it's an obvious conflict of interest for judges to rule on cases involving the citizens whose votes they need to win; it's one of the reasons federal judges are appointed by one branch and approved by another.)

Your city or town probably has a setup with some aspects of the federal and state governments. Think of a mayor and the mayor's office as the executive branch for the city. There are probably some local departments, such as a school board or a parks department. Depending on where you live, the role of the legislative branch might be handled by a city council or a board of supervisors or another group of elected officials.

The county where you live probably has its own elected offices, like county commissioners or a county clerk. There might also be local offices that cover districts instead of cities or counties. Your town might have more than one school district, or one school district might cover a few towns in the area. Even jobs that don't seem political, such as coroner, can be elected offices in certain parts of the country.

In a few places, it's even still possible to literally be elected dogcatcher.

WHAT ALL OF THOSE CHOICES MEAN

As you've probably gathered by now, the government of the United States is a complicated system of institutions with a wide range of responsibilities.

It's not a perfect analogy, but you can think of the layers as a pyramid. The top jobs in Washington have more power over the big picture, but that power exists in a relatively small number of offices. More people serve in state governments, and below them, many, many more serve in municipal and local governments. So in your hometown, you can play a big role in who gets to be mayor or serve on the city council or local board.

As a voter, you only get a say for 2 percent of the Senate and less than 0.23 percent of the House (and if you live in Washington, DC, or the overseas territories, it's a flat 0 percent). Meanwhile, while there are only 535 members of the federal legislature, there are more than *seven thousand* state legislators around the country. As of the 2010 national census, there are a few hundred thousand elected officials in the United States. That's not a typo, and that's just the elected ones, not counting those who were appointed. It also doesn't count any of the officers of political parties, who in some states are elected by the voters who choose to be members of that party.

Just as all these levels of government can pass the laws you need to live by, you get a say in who serves at every level. We'll discuss how in the next few chapters. ■

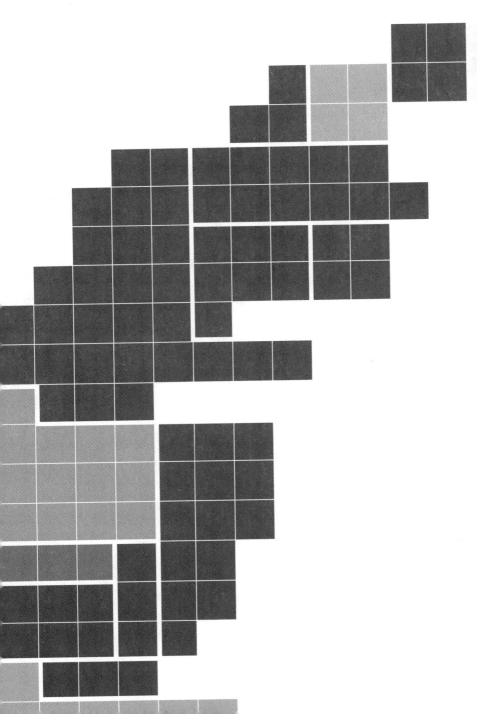

CHAPTER 2

HOW VOTING WORKS

Section I
So Why Vote?

If you finished the last chapter, you'll understand the basics of how the federal government is set up. Some of it's by the design of the founders, some of it's by tradition, and some of it changes as the need arises (it's not the founders' fault that they didn't plan for airport security or how to regulate the internet).

Just like any system, though, how well the government works really depends on the people involved. Here's where you come in.

REASON TO VOTE #1: CIVIC RESPONSIBILITY

Campaigns are basically a job interview, and Election Day is the hiring decision. Other than age and citizenship, there are no specific requirements for becoming the president or a senator or a representative, other than what voters are willing to support. All the campaigning, all the advertising, all the policy statements—at the end of the day, it's about winning.

It's a cliché for candidates to say things like, "If we only had a government as good as our people." Stuff like that usually gets applause on campaign stops (people love being told they're great), but the fact is, the people pick the government. When the government's lousy, that's at least partly the fault of voters for not picking better representatives.

Let's be real. Candidates running for office need to get people to support them. They're going to propose policies that they think will get them more votes than their opponents and explain their positions in a way that makes them sound appealing to as many of their target voters as possible.

It's not unusual to hear cynical complaints about how "all politicians are crooks," or "they don't listen to the people," or dozens of other similar ideas. Are there some politicians who are crooks? Absolutely. Are some too close to lobbyists or industries that donated to the campaign? Definitely. However, there are plenty of people who run for office because they genuinely think they can improve things. More than a few politicians really listen to their constituents and try to make their lives better. The only way the good ones get into office and stay there is by getting more votes than the others. The status quo has a lot of money and resources behind it; the way things change is if people who want to change them (for better or worse) get into office.

Contrary to another cliché, you still technically have the right to complain if you don't vote (after all, it's guaranteed under the First Amendment). It just makes your argument a bit stronger if you did something about it.

REASON TO VOTE #2: MAKING GOVERNMENT BETTER

This doesn't mean it's easy, or that it happens in one election cycle, but voting can influence who runs for office and how they behave once they do it. If candidates who propose real solutions to climate change or the national debt or income inequality consistently do well, more candidates are going to feel comfortable campaigning on those kinds of important issues. Those who already have a plan would be more willing to talk about it, and those who would rather avoid the issues would feel pressure to take a stand.

Anyone who tells you it doesn't matter who's in office is either ignorant of history, lying, or just not thinking before they talk. A lot of things we take for granted—the National Parks, Social Security, Medicare—owe their creation to specific presidents, were once controversial, and now benefit everyone.

More recently, it's pretty unlikely that a president other than George W. Bush would have invaded Iraq, or that Congress would have passed an affordable health insurance program without Barack Obama campaigning on the issue. Few people other than Donald Trump would try to ban Muslim immigrants from several countries, announce plans to pull the United States out of the Paris Climate Accord (joining only Syria outside the agreement), shut down the government for weeks over funding for a border wall, or routinely spread disproven conspiracy theories on Twitter. You can probably find plenty of examples in your state or at your local level when a particular governor or mayor genuinely changed policy.

Getting involved in the process is how citizens hold their representatives accountable. When candidates who pander or appeal to the lowest common denominator do well, they don't really have much incentive to change. It's a lot easier to scare voters about social issues or just campaign on blanket opposition to the other political party than it is to actually govern well and make difficult choices. If your senator, representative, or mayor is doing a good job, vote to reelect them. Don't just assume they're going to win, because their opponents might not get that message. If they're lazy or dishonest or incompetent, find a better option and support them instead. Primaries are a good way to do that, and we'll talk about them shortly.

REASON TO VOTE #3: MAKING YOUR VOICE HEARD

If that doesn't make you feel inspired or guilty enough to get involved, look at it this way: the very fact that you're able to vote is a sign of progress.

Remember, when the United States was new, most states (and it's the states—not the federal government—that have always had control over voting) only let (mostly white) men who owned land vote. Expanding voting rights was always a struggle, because the officials in charge had, by definition, benefited from the way things were; the way things were put them in office.

Popular movements obviously played a big role, and it sometimes took activists decades of work, but eventually enough members of Congress and enough state legislators were convinced to pass and ratify the constitutional amendments covered in the last chapter. An eighteen-year-old African American woman in 1800 could have been denied the vote because of her age, her race, or her gender. Untold numbers of Americans sacrificed so that today it's illegal to deny the same citizen the vote for any of those reasons. It's hard to deny that expanding voting rights to more citizens has changed the country—and changed it for the better.

Keep in mind that while the federal government outlaws many forms of discrimination in voting, citizens don't technically have a federal right to vote, and some states handle that right differently.

We'll talk about that later in the book, when we cover how to vote (chapter 4). First, we'll take a look at how elections work, starting with the big prize—the presidential election.

Section II
Picking the President

On the surface, the presidential election can seem relatively simple. It's the only election in which every eligible voter in the country can take part. It's always held on a predictable schedule—the first Tuesday after the first Monday in November. (In other words, between November 2 and November 8.) It's the world's most talked-about and most expensive election.

Of course, there's more to it than that. The US presidential election operates differently from that of any other nation.

THE ELECTORAL COLLEGE

One uniquely American compromise is that citizens don't vote for the president. At least, not technically. Instead, when you go to your polling place on Election Day, you're actually voting for a team of electors whose names you probably don't recognize but who will cast an official ballot for the president a few weeks later.

The Electoral College started as another compromise by the members of the Constitutional Convention, and—just like the other compromises they negotiated—it was what the framers could agree to live with, rather than what any side truly wanted. They didn't want Congress or state legislatures to pick the president, figuring that would make corruption and dealmaking too easy. But they also didn't want a direct election, worried that voters would just go with local candidates and, therefore, only elect candidates from states with a lot of people (good for New York, but not so good for Delaware). Many of them also didn't trust that the citizens would always make informed choices. Even if they never had to use it, they wanted a safeguard against a dangerous selection.

So they again set up a system that was democratic only up to a point, with each state choosing electors—anyone except federal employees or members of Congress is eligible to be an elector—who would vote on behalf of everyone in the state. To make small states happy, the framers agreed to give each state one elector for every senator (since each state has two) and one for each representative (so the big states would still go for it). Those electors would then get one vote each, and the candidate with a majority would win. Today, with fifty states and the District of Columbia voting, it takes 270 electoral votes out of a possible 538 to become president.

Originally, each state was allowed to pick its electors its own way, and most just had the state legislature do it. Easy, but not so democratic. Eventually, one by one, states realized it made a lot more sense for the people to vote for president and have the electors vote the same way.

Today, each state's political parties choose their possible electors the summer before Election Day. Some states will list those electors on the November ballot; others just list the candidates. Either way, if you vote Democratic, you're actually voting for Democratic electors chosen by the Democratic Party who will later vote for the Democratic candidate.

THE LANDSLIDE EFFECT

Because the Electoral College makes nearly every state a winner-take-all prize, the electoral vote totals can make races look a lot less close than they actually were.

For example:

1964

POPULAR VOTE: Lyndon Johnson (61.1 percent), Barry Goldwater (38.5 percent)

ELECTORAL VOTE: Johnson 486, Goldwater 52

1980

POPULAR VOTE: Ronald Reagan (50.7 percent), Jimmy Carter (41.0 percent), John Anderson (6.6 percent)

ELECTORAL VOTE: Reagan 489, Carter 49, Anderson 0*

1984

POPULAR VOTE: Ronald Reagan (58.8 percent), Walter Mondale (40.6 percent)

ELECTORAL VOTE: Reagan 525, Mondale 13

1992

POPULAR VOTE: Bill Clinton (43.0 percent), George H. W. Bush (37.5 percent), Ross Perot (18.9 percent)

ELECTORAL VOTE: Clinton 370, Bush 168, Perot 0**

*This is why third-party candidates hate the Electoral College (more on them on page 122).

**This too.

WHEN THE ELECTORAL COLLEGE DOESN'T WORK

A system this complicated was bound to have problems. For one thing, a candidate can win the popular vote and lose the electoral vote, meaning the person most Americans want to be president doesn't become the president. And that's happened. A few times.

Rutherford B. Hayes (1876), Benjamin Harrison (1888), George W. Bush (2000), and Donald Trump (2016) managed to lose their elections but win the presidency anyway (a pretty good consolation prize) by getting enough Electoral College votes. Twice, nobody won a majority of the Electoral College, so the House of Representatives had to pick the president (Thomas Jefferson in 1800 and John Quincy Adams in 1824).

During a presidential election year, you'll hear about national polls that show what percentages of all voters are expected to support one candidate or the other. The Electoral College means that doesn't necessarily matter. In 2000 it all came down to a legal fight over counting Florida's electoral votes, with whoever won the state becoming president. Even though Vice President Al Gore won more than half a million more votes than Texas governor George W. Bush did nationwide, it took more than a month before the presidency was determined because Florida's results weren't decided.

In the 2016 election, the difference between the popular and electoral votes made the 2000 result look normal by comparison. Former New York senator and US secretary of state Hillary Clinton outpaced businessman and reality-show star Donald Trump by about 2.9 million votes—more than five times Gore's margin against Bush—to take 48.5 percent of the vote to his 46.4 percent. While the Electoral College went 271–266 for Bush

"You win some, you lose some. And then there's that little-known third category."

—AL GORE, AFTER WINNING THE POPULAR VOTE IN 2000 BUT LOSING THE PRESIDENCY AFTER A SUPREME COURT BATTLE

in 2000, small margins in several states made the 2016 election night total a more lopsided 306–232 against the candidate with more votes.

Also, in more than twenty states, the electors don't actually have to vote the way the state's voters want. These rogues are called *faithless electors*, and they have switched votes 157 times. The first, in 1796, switched from John Adams to Thomas Jefferson in a close election (Jefferson lost by only three electoral votes), but nearly half of faithless electors switched because the candidate they were supposed to support died before the Electoral College voted. In 2016 seven electors broke ranks, costing Clinton five votes and Trump two. (The beneficiaries? Three votes went to former secretary of state Colin Powell, and one vote each went to Ohio governor John Kasich, Vermont senator Bernie Sanders, former Texas congressman Ron Paul, and activist Faith Spotted Eagle.) Plus, faithless electors from Washington state gave vice-presidential votes to four women who didn't run for the job.

You can probably see why a lot of people want to get rid of the Electoral College. But it's in the Constitution, which means it will take an amendment to change it—and with the extra power it gives small states, those small states will never agree to that. (Forty of the fifty states have fewer people than Los Angeles

County alone, so you can see why it'd be hard to convince the required thirty-eight of them to ratify a change.) So far, Congress has introduced more than seven hundred plans to reform or eliminate the college. There have been more proposed amendments dealing with the electoral vote than any other subject in US history, but none have gone anywhere.

THE RED AND THE BLUE

One of the best arguments against the Electoral College is that it forces presidential candidates to spend a lot of effort campaigning in *swing states*—states where neither Democrats nor Republicans make up an obvious majority of voters—and ignore the states they know they're going to win or lose.

After the 2000 election, the political divide in the United States became known as a country of *red states* and *blue states*, based on which color the TV news networks used to indicate the states that voted for Bush and Gore, respectively. (The colors on the network maps used to alternate between the parties; only after 2000 did each color become permanently identified with one party.)

It's an oversimplification—especially when talking about races other than the presidential one—but the red state versus blue state idea is useful to illustrate how candidates campaign. As you can guess, the need to appeal to certain states can be a serious factor in what issues get talked about during the campaign. It also has a lot to do with where candidates spend their time and where they spend their money.

If you live in a solidly red or blue state, particularly one without a big population, you can easily go through an entire general

COLLEGE EDUCATION

Maine and Nebraska are the only states that don't automatically give all their electoral votes to one candidate, instead dividing them based on congressional districts. In 2016 Maine gave three votes to Hillary Clinton and one to Donald Trump, the first time it split since that became an option in 1972. Nebraska last split in 2008, giving John McCain four votes and Barack Obama one.

In theory, a candidate can get the 270 votes needed to become president by winning just twelve states. The catch? Those states must include California, Texas, New York, Florida, Illinois, Pennsylvania, and Ohio (the other five can be mixed, as long as either New Jersey or Michigan is among them).

Even though the District of Columbia has three electoral votes, thanks to the Twenty-Third Amendment, American citizens in other nonstate territories—including Puerto Rico, American Samoa, the US Virgin Islands, Guam, and the Northern Mariana Islands—don't get any say on Election Day.

election without either presidential candidate even visiting. You'll avoid seeing constant presidential ads if you watch TV in prime-time (you'll still get local political ads), but unfortunately, it's because your state simply isn't a priority in the presidential election. Heavily populated states that aren't "purple" might get a little attention, but it's the swing states that really get the love.

For example, take the 2012 presidential election. The *Washington Post* broke down how often President Barack Obama and Republican challenger Mitt Romney visited each state between

June and the November election. Voters in several states, including the line of states from North Dakota south to Oklahoma, never had a chance to meet either of them during that time. Even if you throw in the candidates' wives and vice-presidential running mates, Kansas, Alaska, and North Dakota were seen as too clearly Republican, and Hawaii, Vermont, and Maine too clearly Democratic, to earn a visit.

In a state both candidates think they can win, they'll show up and campaign for your vote. Quite often, in fact. Using the 2012 example again, Ohio hosted 47 visits from Governor Romney and 29 from President Obama. (Make that 148 total visits, including their spouses and running mates.) Florida received 115 visits, including 38 from Romney and 26 from Obama.

States don't necessarily stay red or blue. Whether because of changing demographics, people moving into or out of certain states, or the appeal of particular candidates, the Electoral College map looks very different now than it did a few decades ago, and it will probably look just as different a few decades into the future. During the 2008 election, Barack Obama's landslide victory against John McCain included winning states like Indiana, Virginia, and North Carolina, which no Democratic presidential candidate had won in decades, and sweeping all of the states considered swing states that year. In 2016 Hillary Clinton's defeat hinged on close losses in three longtime blue states, as she became the first Democrat to lose Pennsylvania since 1984 and the first to lose Michigan and Wisconsin since 1988. (Clinton's decision not to visit Wisconsin all year received a lot of attention after she lost the state by only about twenty-three thousand votes, though widespread voter suppression was a bigger factor. See sidebar on page 140.)

In a state that definitely isn't going to swing, it can feel like your vote doesn't matter—and in the presidential election, that can be true. Still, the people who show up to vote can make a larger impact in any number of other races on the same ballot.

Depending on the state, even ones that aren't competitive in November, it's also possible to have a say in the presidential election months before the final vote, thanks to primaries.

Section III
The Primaries

Before the Democratic nominee, Republican nominee, and any third-party nominees face off in November, voters have to decide who those nominees are going to be. That happens in primary elections.

You can make an argument that voting in primaries is actually more important than voting in the general election. Once it comes down to the final choice, the vast majority of Democratic voters are going to vote for the Democratic nominee, and the vast majority of Republican voters will do exactly the same thing for the Republican nominee.

Primaries are how those nominees are chosen, and it's not that unusual to see underdog candidates succeed and front-runners collapse (see sidebar on page 72). Rather than a national, winner-take-all election, primaries take place state by state. No matter how much one candidate is expected to win,

POLLS THAT DON'T MATTER

During every presidential election cycle, news channels will air stories that make a big deal about who's winning in the national polls before primaries even start. That can be infuriating, because when elections are decided state by state, national polls simply don't matter.

For pretty much all of 2007, several polls consistently predicted a 2008 presidential matchup between New York senator Hillary Clinton and former New York City mayor Rudy Giuliani. Neither one won a nomination. (Clinton at least finished a respectable second to Barack Obama; Giuliani won as many primaries as you did, despite spending a lot more money.)

In 2003 many polls showed Senator Joe Lieberman, at the time the Democratic Party's most recent vice-presidential nominee, leading the nine candidates for the 2004 Democratic nomination. (He awkwardly called it "Joementum" but didn't keep it going long enough to win a single primary.)

There are a few reasons why polls like these can be so misleading. First, early polls are mostly about name recognition, because voters who aren't political junkies haven't really started to pay attention to the race yet. As governors or senators who aren't yet national household names continue to campaign, they get more attention, and that can mean more support. Also, early primaries affect the others. If candidates do well in Iowa and New Hampshire, they get more news coverage, more people become aware of them, and voters start to feel like they could win. Finishing second in four early primaries can be more disastrous for a campaign than finishing last in two and winning two. Plus, as primary season goes along, candidates drop out of the race, and most of their supporters choose one of the remaining candidates.

a few victories in early primaries can completely change the dynamics of the race.

In 2008, in an election without a sitting president running, Democratic voters had the opportunity to pick between eight declared candidates, and Republicans chose from their own slate of eight candidates. When the same situation occurred in 2016, Democrats had three choices and Republicans a whopping twelve. In both those elections, a few other candidates dropped out of the race before the first primary. Some people still complain that they don't like their choices, but the upside of primaries is they make sure voters at least *have* choices. The downside of the system is that, because voting is done state by state, the race is often decided before a number of states have a chance to vote.

Much as voting for president on Election Day is actually voting for electors who will vote for president, voting in a Democratic or Republican presidential primary is voting for delegates to that party's national convention, where the party nominee is officially chosen.

BEFORE PRIMARIES EXISTED

Though they're incredibly important now, primaries are a relatively new thing. Even once they were created, it took some time before they truly mattered. The good news is that primaries give voters much, much more say in who the parties nominate— especially because, in the beginning, voters basically had no say.

Political parties are now a permanent part of American politics, and for most of our history there have usually been two dominant ones. Since 1854, those have been the Democratic Party and the Republican Party. The two-party system feels so normal to us that it's worth mentioning that the Constitution doesn't say anything about political parties. Still, once George Washington announced he wasn't going to seek a third term, partisan presidential politics sprang up, with John Adams and Thomas Jefferson running against each other in 1796. (We'll talk more about parties in the next chapter.)

Originally, the party nominees were just chosen by some members of the parties in Congress, who got together and decided who should run. It wasn't a terribly formal process, and the public didn't know how the nominees were picked or why; they were just given a choice between the parties' nominees.

By 1824, the country had gotten bigger. Congress had also gotten bigger, and the less-than-democratic nature of the nomination system seemed ripe for reform. It took an unusual election to force the change.

That year, the congressional caucus of the Democratic-Republican Party—the only major political party at the time—nominated William Crawford for president. Between his selection and the election, Crawford suffered complications from a stroke, and it seemed like he might not be able to do the job. Crawford's health problems caused a few other candidates to jump into the race, and nobody received a majority of the popular vote or of the Electoral College. The decision fell to the House of Representatives, which chose John Quincy Adams as president, even though Andrew Jackson had performed better in both the popular vote (41.4 percent to 30.9 percent) and the electoral vote (99 to 84).

Jackson developed a rather large chip on his shoulder about the result. After he won a rematch with Adams four years later, the brief one-party rule of the country was toast. Jackson's supporters formed the modern Democratic Party, while his political opponents created the Whig Party. And in 1832, the Democrats held a national convention, the next stage in how American parties would pick their presidential candidates.

FROM CONVENTIONS TO PRIMARIES

Soon the national conventions became the most important events on the political calendar before Election Day, and the parties truly didn't know who their nominees would be until the convention delegates decided. Starting in 1832, the Democrats began a tradition of bringing together delegates from every state and having them vote for the presidential and vice-presidential nominees. The Whigs followed suit a few years later, and the Republican Party did the same thing once it replaced the Whigs as the second major party.

This was at least a little more democratic, since every state was represented at conventions, and the delegates had to vote on as many ballots as it took until a nominee received two-thirds of the vote. On the other hand, it still allowed powerful party bosses to trade favors and influence delegates to vote the way they wanted. By the late 1800s, this kind of boss-run politics (or *machine politics*) was a real problem in both parties and in many parts of the country. At the same time, the Industrial Revolution had created massive income inequality, dangerous working conditions, and overpopulated cities.

Activists and journalists called for reform, and some politicians in both parties introduced solutions to these problems. These good-government reforms of the late 1800s and early 1900s, known as

AN UNCONVENTIONAL CONVENTION

The 1968 primary was a worst-case scenario for the Democratic Party.

Despite an impressive record on domestic policy, President Lyndon Johnson's expansion of the conflict in Vietnam had made him unpopular with many Democratic voters. So much so that, with anti-war senator Eugene McCarthy winning early primaries and Senator Robert F. Kennedy also joining the race, the president announced in March that he wouldn't seek reelection. Kennedy looked like the next nominee, but he was assassinated at a campaign event in Los Angeles on June 6, the same night that he won the California primary.

At the party convention in Chicago that August, Kennedy's supporters split among multiple candidates. Delegates went with the seemingly safe choice, Vice President Hubert Humphrey, even though he hadn't won any primaries. Meanwhile, thousands of anti-war protesters demonstrated outside the convention and were attacked by the Chicago police and the National Guard. As protesters put it, the whole world was watching, as news cameras captured the beatings and tear gas. The police riots became a

....

the Progressive Era, included the introduction of antitrust laws to break up monopolies, as well as income taxes, women's suffrage, and anti-corruption reforms. The Seventeenth Amendment, which allowed voters to choose their own senators (instead of state legislatures doing it for them) was another example of these reforms.

So was the notion of a *preference primary*, an election in which voters could select their delegates to the convention based on who those delegates would support for president. In 1910 Oregon was

Protesters and members of the National Guard face off outside the 1968
Democratic Convention in Chicago.

bigger news story than the Democrats choosing a nominee. That
nightmare, combined with Humphrey's eventual loss to Richard
Nixon, gave reformers the opportunity they needed to make the
nomination process more democratic.

the first state to create this kind of primary, and a dozen states had
one by the 1912 election.

These primaries weren't binding—delegates could still change
their minds during the rounds of voting at the convention—but at
least voters, instead of state party leaders, were able to choose who
the states sent to those conventions. Between 1912 and 1968, though,
only a minority of states established primaries, and the number de-
creased from a peak of twenty to only twelve states by 1968.

However, after the chaos of the 1968 Democratic National Convention (see sidebar on page 76), both parties moved to make the primary process itself the point, with the convention losing importance. Just one election cycle later, there was a true role reversal, and voters in states around the country were telling the party leaders which candidates to nominate.

THE PRIMARY SYSTEM

From 1972 onward, both major parties gradually increased the number of primaries and caucuses. The two parties' primary systems are similar but not exactly the same. For example, some states have both the Democratic and Republican primaries on the same day, while others hold them separately. The Democratic Party awards its delegates proportionally in every state, while the Republican Party allows states to have a "winner takes all" system if they choose (as the name suggests, the winner of the primary receives all of the state's delegates). That means the Democratic race tends to stay competitive longer, while a Republican can finish a close second over and over without winning any delegates.

Both parties also have *superdelegates*, or high-ranking party officials who are automatic delegates to the convention, though superdelegates make up a larger percentage of the Democratic delegation. (Former presidents, former senators, and former serious contenders for the nomination are usually among them.) On the Democratic side, they can vote for whichever candidate they want. That means early primary coverage will often count them in the total delegates won to date (which helps front-runners look dominant), though they can change their minds whenever they

KEEPING ORDER

By voting early, Iowa and New Hampshire hold the kind of influence other states would love to have. Though states pick their primary dates, national Democratic and Republican leaders try to keep states from changing the schedule too dramatically.

In 2008 Michigan decided to move its primary up to January 15, jumping ahead of South Carolina and Nevada, even though the national parties had placed those states next in line following Iowa and New Hampshire.

Both parties decided to punish Michigan, vowing not to seat the state's delegates at the convention. Most of the viable Democratic candidates pulled their names off the ballot (Hillary Clinton didn't and won the vote), and candidates from both parties avoided serious campaigning in the state.

The lesson? States have some control over when they vote for president, but not unlimited control.

....

want. However, the party decided in 2018 not to let them vote at the convention any longer, unless they're needed to break a tie. On the Republican side, since 2012 superdelegates have been required to vote the way their state's primary voters did, which led to many who opposed Donald Trump throughout 2016 either voting for him or skipping the convention.

Those differences aside, the general idea of a primary is the same. In one state after another, voters select their preferences, and the candidates pick up delegates for the convention. Since this system went into effect, the party usually knows who the presidential nominee will be well ahead of the convention, and the nominee selects his or her own vice-presidential nominee.

There are three main forms of primary elections. Some states have open primaries, which means any voter can take a ballot in either the Republican or Democratic election (but not both), without being affiliated with any party. Others are closed, meaning you need to register as a member of the party to vote in its primary. Still others have a semiclosed system, in which unaffiliated voters can choose either party primary, but affiliated voters can't switch. In a few states, the two parties use different systems.

By tradition, the first two contests are the Iowa caucuses and the New Hampshire primary, which usually take place in January or February. It is possible for a candidate to win the nomination while losing both of those votes—Bill Clinton pulled that off in 1992 and went on to become president, but nobody else did it from 1972 to 2016. So while losing both states doesn't end a campaign, it can put a candidate in a tight spot early in the election cycle.

The caucus system used in Iowa functions differently from a standard election. Instead of voters going to a polling place and casting a ballot, they attend caucus meetings around the state. People at each caucus have a chance to tell the other attendees why they support their preferred candidate, and then the group votes. The parties have separate caucuses and their rules are different, but both are electing delegates to county conventions, where the delegates will eventually pick Iowa's delegates to the national convention—the caucus itself doesn't decide the final number of delegates each candidate receives.

That makes Iowa sound less important than it is. How candidates do in Iowa will always be a big news story. Finishing better than expected can give candidates national attention and some momentum for the next race. If campaigns really try to win Iowa but perform poorly, that sometimes reveals enough problems with the campaign that the candidate drops out of the race early. Candidates can win the nomination without winning Iowa—Bill Clinton, Michael Dukakis, George McGovern, John McCain, Donald Trump, and George H. W. Bush all did it—but winning is definitely helpful.

New Hampshire state law ensures that the state will always hold its primary before any other state does (if another state moves its primary earlier, New Hampshire will move its up in response), and both major parties have gone along with that. Until Bill Clinton in 1992, everyone who won the presidency since 1972 also won his party's New Hampshire primary. However, George W. Bush in 2000 and Barack Obama in 2008 won their elections after losing that primary.

After the Granite State, a series of other states vote, as candidates try to secure enough delegates to ensure they'll win the nomination. South Carolina's primary and Nevada's caucuses follow (Nevada comes first for Democrats, South Carolina for Republicans, and then the reverse). For 2016, those were the only states that voted before Super Tuesday, the nickname for the day that features the greatest number of primaries.

Super Tuesday usually comes in early March (on March 3 in 2020), and the sheer number of states voting that day can often decide the nominee. That decision doesn't become official until the convention, but the winner can still be the presumptive nominee. Candidates who are too far behind after that point often drop out of the race, because it's hard to catch up and they've usually spent a lot of money on the early states. Other times, Super Tuesday simply cuts the field down to a smaller number of contenders, who fight for votes in a few more states.

The largest and earliest Super Tuesday in American history so far came in 2008, when twenty-four states—representing more than half of the convention delegates—moved their primaries all the way up to February 5. On the Democratic side, Barack Obama outperformed Hillary Clinton, but not by a large enough margin for her to drop out. He led the rest of the way, but the race continued through June 5, the end of the primary schedule. On the Republican side, John McCain won enough delegates on Super Tuesday that his closest challenger, Mitt Romney, withdrew from the race two days later.

That was a strange case, because for the first time since 1952, neither party had a sitting president or a vice president running, and both races were (rightly, it turned out) expected to be unusually competitive when the states were scheduling their primaries. Four years later, Super Tuesday was back to its normal slot in early March.

Presidential primaries continue even once there's a presumptive nominee (and the same primary process picks party nominees for other offices). All fifty states have either a primary or a caucus. So do the territories, like Puerto Rico and American Samoa, which don't get a say in the Electoral College but do send delegates to the conventions and elect their own local officials.

Like a lot of the American governmental system, the primary schedule has its pluses and minuses.

On the minus side, as noted earlier, the front-loaded schedule means the nominees are often decided before voters in a fair number of states ever get a chance to vote. Also, Iowa and New Hampshire are not the most demographically diverse of states, so there's an argument to be made that the process could be more representative.

On the plus side, having a few small states vote first evens the playing field among the candidates a little bit. Because Iowa and New Hampshire are relatively small, candidates have a chance to speak to and meet with a fairly high percentage of voters. Because they spend a lot of time in at least one of those two states (and usually both), candidates can rely on face-to-face "retail politics" instead of expensive ads to get their message out, and everyone has about the same amount of time to spend (which generally isn't true of money).

If you live in an early primary or caucus state, odds are good that you'll have more say in the election during the primary than in November. For the rest of you, primaries are still important, and the presidential candidates aren't the only ones selected through them.

Section IV
Picking Congress

In the last chapter, we covered some of the differences between the Senate and the House of Representatives, in terms of how the two houses are made up and how they pass laws.

The two houses also have very different elections.

Members of the House are elected to two-year terms, and they all run in every national election. Every two years, the entire

REPLACING A CANDIDATE

To get a sense of how differently state laws can treat similar situations, consider these two Senate races from the early 2000s.

In 2000 the outgoing Democratic governor of Missouri, Mel Carnahan, was running for the US Senate when he died in a plane crash on October 6, less than a month before the election. Under Missouri law, the party wasn't allowed to replace him on the ballot, so voters could either elect the late governor or his opponent, incumbent Republican John Ashcroft. If Carnahan won, the lieutenant governor—who took over as governor after the crash—would be able to appoint a replacement for two years and promised to appoint Carnahan's wife, Jean. That's what happened. The dead governor won the Senate election against Ashcroft by about 2 percent, and his widow served a two-year term in the Senate.

Two years later, incumbent Democratic senator Paul Wellstone of Minnesota also died in a plane crash while campaigning on October 25, even closer to the election. Unlike Missouri, Minnesota required the party to replace Wellstone on the ballot. Democrats turned to former vice president and 1984 presidential candidate Walter Mondale, who lost a close vote to Republican Norm Coleman on November 5.

House of Representatives can be swapped out, and the party in power can be replaced by a pretty large margin. The first part hasn't happened (while people often complain about Congress overall, they usually reelect their own representatives), but there have been some pretty substantial swings in who runs Congress.

In the most extreme example, in 1894, 111 seats changed party in one day (and there were only 357 members of the House at the time, instead of 435).

The Senate, on the other hand, can never be replaced all at once. Senators are elected to six-year terms, and only about one third of the Senate runs for election at the same time. Senate seats are assigned to one of three classes, and those groups take turns.

That was a little tricky in the beginning, when members of the first Senate were divided into Class 1, Class 2, and Class 3. The senators were divided into three equal groups, and they drew numbers to see who was up for reelection when (remember, state legislatures still chose senators at that time). After the first three election cycles, the process became more streamlined, with each class serving six years. There have been seven elections in which more than ten Senate seats changed from one party to the other, with a record eighteen in 1866, just after the Civil War. The way the classes are set up, the two senators for each state are in different classes, so barring special circumstances, voters don't replace both of their senators at once.

There are exceptions when a senator is replaced in the middle of his or her term. That can happen because they resigned, died, or took a higher-up job in the cabinet. In fact, in some states, it's possible to run for president or vice president at the same time as a Senate run. In 2008 Joe Biden was elected vice president and reelected to his Senate seat from Delaware. He gave up the Senate seat, and the governor nominated a replacement. In 2000 Joe Lieberman ran for vice president and was reelected senator from Connecticut. Though he didn't get to be veep, he stayed in the Senate for twelve more years. When a senator leaves office during a term, depending on the state, either a special election is held for voters to fill the seat or the governor appoints a replacement. Either way, the replacement serves a shorter-than-normal term (usually two years) instead of the full six years (see sidebar on page 84).

CONTROL OF CONGRESS

What that all means is that every four years in November, on the day the country picks the president, it also picks all 435 members of the House and about one third of the Senate. Presidential elections have better voter turnout than elections in other years, which means more people also vote in the Senate and House elections held during presidential years.

If a presidential candidate is particularly popular, that popularity usually helps members of the same party running for other offices, a phenomenon called the *coattails effect* (as in, the down-ballot candidates are carried along by holding on to the presidential candidate's coattails).

When you vote in November, you can vote straight ticket (choosing candidates from the same party for all offices) or split your ticket (choosing candidates from more than one party, such as voting for a Democratic president and a Republican senator).

As partisan as Americans can be, ticket splitting isn't unusual. For example, Indiana never supported a Democrat for president between 1964 and 2008, but three Indiana Democrats combined to win five Senate elections during that time. In 2012, five Democratic senators won seats in states where Mitt Romney defeated Barack Obama.

The entire House of Representatives and another third of the Senate run two years after the presidential election (and two years before the next one), also in November. These *midterm* elections tend to have much lower voter turnout, and that's usually bad news for the president's party. Voters who are unhappy with the president are more likely to show up for midterms, while supporters of the president's party notoriously struggle to get voters to turn out.

In 1934, two years into Democrat Franklin Delano Roosevelt's first term as president, the Democrats managed to gain nine House seats and nine Senate seats. It took another sixty-four years before a president's party gained House seats in a midterm. It happened halfway through Bill Clinton's second term, when Republicans in Congress made the unpopular decision to impeach the president, and voters turned on them. Senate seats are usually less volatile than House seats, but the president usually suffers there, too, during midterms. The president's party has only gained seats in the Senate during five midterm elections since 1934 and has never gained more than three seats.

The biggest midterm drubbing a president's party ever took was in 1938, during FDR's second term, when the Democrats lost seventy-one House seats. But their majority was so big going into the election that they still kept control of the House. In the Senate, the biggest loss was the Republicans dropping thirteen seats in 1958, during Dwight Eisenhower's second term (the only election that included Alaska but not Hawaii, putting the Senate at ninety-eight members).

As we discussed in the last chapter, as much as voters focus on the president, who controls Congress can be just as important when it comes to national policy. Just because midterms don't get as much national attention doesn't mean you should overlook them.

Primaries matter here too. Just as you vote for your party's presidential nominee, you also vote for its House nominees and (if one's running that year) Senate nominee. In some states, that happens on the same day. In others, it might be a separate primary or caucus. (Here, too, nonpresidential elections tend to have lower turnout.)

It's worth pointing out that the third branch of the federal government, the courts, doesn't really apply here. The only say voters have about federal judges is voting for the president who appoints them and the senators who confirm them. That might be a factor in how you vote in those other races—after all, the judges could be in office much longer than the president or senator in question—but that's all you can really do about the federal judiciary.

That covers the federal government, but there's more to note before we move on.

Section V
State and Local Elections

In a theme that's going to come up a lot in this book, don't forget about state and local elections.

State elections are also held on the first Tuesday after the first Monday in November, but it's up to each state to decide when it elects its own officials. Midterm elections are the most popular choice for picking the governor, and there's a logic to that—state governments are the ones making the call, and using the midterm schedule makes the head of the state government the highest-profile office on the ballot. A handful of states use off-year elections, when not even members of Congress are running (see sidebar on page 93).

The different statewide officials elected in most states, such as attorney general and secretary of state, will also appear on the ballot. On your state's Election Day, you can also vote for your state representatives, state senators, and any judges elected in your state. That means even if the presidential or Senate race in your state isn't going to be close, there can still be any number of competitive races, and the outcome of them can have consequences for you and your friends and family.

Also, never assume that your state being red or blue on the presidential map means down-ballot races automatically favor one party. It isn't a far-fetched scenario that a state would vote one way for president and another for governor; it happens all the time. Massachusetts is generally considered one of the most Democratic states in the country, and hasn't voted for a Republican presidential candidate since 1984—but from 1990 to 2014, it chose Republican governors five out of seven times. Montana is solidly Republican in presidential races, but supported Democratic candidates in its 2004, 2008, 2012, and 2016 gubernatorial elections.

There's a good reason for that. The candidates nominated for state office by political parties—both the leadership of the parties and the rank-and-file voters who take part in the primary—live in that state, know its unique concerns, and only need to

PRIMARY AS A VERB

In the last few election cycles, Senate primaries—primarily, pardon the pun, on the Republican side—have seen more unexpected upsets than usual. With lower turnout than the general election, it's been easier for organized groups to mobilize and replace incumbent senators with new nominees, a process now called *primarying*.

This has created a dilemma for Republicans, as conservative activists defeated longtime senators including Richard Lugar (Indiana) and Robert Bennett (Utah), as well as would-be Senate candidates who were popular statewide, such as Heather Wilson (New Mexico) and Mike Castle (Delaware)—replacing each of them with nominees further to the political right.

In 2017 Alabama senator Luther Strange, who was appointed when Jefferson Beauregard Sessions III left the Senate to become US attorney general, lost a Republican primary to ultraconservative

appeal to voters in that state. A voter can, for example, agree with one party's approach to domestic issues but not its views on foreign policy, making the choice much easier in a gubernatorial race than in a presidential one. Generally (though not always), a Democrat running in a very red state is going to be more conservative on some issues than a Democrat running for president, and a Republican running in a very blue state will be more liberal on some issues than his or her presidential equivalent. It's a bit of a chicken-and-egg scenario—do the candidate's politics reflect their home state, or does appealing to voters in that state change their politics?—but it's a common one.

former judge Roy Moore. Moore's extremist views (he was twice removed from his role as a judge because he refused to comply with federal law), combined with accusations of sexual assault or inappropriate advances from nine women (some of whom were underage at the time of the incidents) gave Democrats a chance to win a seat in a state so red that Sessions was the only candidate on the ballot in 2014. Former prosecutor Doug Jones defeated Moore in a close race, racking up the first Democratic Senate win in Alabama since 1992.

To the activists responsible, these races were a way to make the party move further to the right, which was their goal. For the party leadership, this was a headache, as it cost Republicans seats in the general election that they probably could have won (or at least come closer to winning) with more mainstream candidates.

Just as with federal offices, nominees for many key state offices also need to win primaries in advance of the general election. The three categories of primaries and caucuses that states use for federal races—open, closed, and semiclosed—can all apply at the state level.

A handful of states use different rules for their primaries (remember, these examples don't apply to the presidential primary).

Alaska is the only state to use a blanket primary for state offices, and it applies to every party except the Republicans (who have their own semiclosed primary). During the blanket primary, all candidates appear on the same ballot, and the top vote getter for each party then appears on the November ballot. Blanket primaries used to be more common, but in 2000 the Supreme Court ruled they're unconstitutional unless the parties don't object (in Alaska, only the GOP objected).

Washington and California use *top-two* primary systems. All candidates for an office appear on the same primary ballot, and the two top finishers face off in November. In practice, that still favors the major parties if they each promote one primary candidate, but it can allow candidates from smaller parties to have a better shot at getting into the final two. (Nebraska uses a similar system for choosing its state legislature but not other offices.) In California in 2016, the top two spots in the primary to replace retiring senator Barbara Boxer went to a pair of Democrats, Kamala Harris and Loretta Sanchez, with Harris prevailing in the November rematch.

Louisiana has a unique system, as the only one of the fifty states without a primary or caucus to pick nominees. Instead, every candidate runs on the same ballot in November. If one candidate gets more than half the vote, he or she wins the election. If not, the top two finishers—regardless of their party—face each other in a runoff in December.

Local elections (mayor, school board, local bond issues, etc.) have even more variety. They obviously need to comply with state law, but they don't have to follow the state's election schedule. Big cities, including the country's five biggest metropolises—New York City, Los Angeles, Chicago, Houston, and Philadelphia—usually hold their mayoral elections in off years. Those are cities with resources, and their races can attract big-name candidates and solid voter turnout.

COMING TO TERMS

States have three options for when they pick their governors, and most governors serve four-year terms.

Presidential Year

Eleven states elect their governors at the same time the country's electing a president (2012, 2016, 2020, 2024, etc.).

Delaware, Indiana, Missouri, Montana, New Hampshire,* North Carolina, North Dakota, Utah, Vermont,* Washington, and West Virginia

Midterm

Thirty-six states vote for the state's top job when Congress and one third of the Senate, but not the president, are being selected (2014, 2018, 2022, 2026, etc.).

Alabama, Alaska, Arizona, Arkansas, California, Colorado, Connecticut, Florida, Georgia, Hawaii, Idaho, Illinois, Iowa, Kansas, Maine, Maryland, Massachusetts, Michigan, Minnesota, Nebraska, Nevada, New Hampshire,* New Mexico, New York, Ohio, Oklahoma, Oregon, Pennsylvania, Rhode Island, South Carolina, South Dakota, Tennessee, Texas, Vermont,* Wisconsin, and Wyoming

Off-Year

Five states elect governors separately from national elections, but not all at the same time.

New Jersey and Virginia (2009, 2013, 2017, 2021, etc.)
Kentucky, Louisiana, and Mississippi (2011, 2015, 2019, 2023, etc.)

*New Hampshire and Vermont elect their governors every two years.

SCHEDULE CONCERNS

It's rare for elections to be postponed and rescheduled, but that can happen in extraordinary circumstances.

September 11, 2001, will forever be remembered for the attacks carried out by al-Qaeda terrorists—particularly in New York City, the site of the destroyed World Trade Center. Understandably less remembered is that September 11, 2001, was also the day of the Democratic and Republican primaries for the city's mayor. Knowing it would be almost impossible to carry out a fair vote that day, Governor George Pataki made the decision to postpone the election a few hours after the polls opened. The primaries were instead held two weeks later, on September 25, while the November 6 general election stayed the same.

Though the Constitution doesn't say so, in theory, Congress has the power to postpone an election if it must. In 2004 the House passed a resolution saying it would never postpone the federal election because of a terrorist attack. (What to do about the other likely threat—a natural disaster such as a hurricane, tornado, or earthquake—is still an open question.)

Smaller cities and localities are more likely to hold local votes during presidential years or midterm years. If a town, village, or county needs to set up polling places and register voters anyway, it's cheaper, and easier in terms of staffing and logistics, to piggyback on a federal election than to hold one during an off year. Plus, turnout is almost always higher for an election held during a presidential year. (That can be seen as a negative by local officials with loyal followers who turn out in off years, when other voters are probably going to stay home.)

Whether local elections involve a primary, which offices are up for election when, whether candidates run with or without a party affiliation, what happens if nobody wins a majority—all these kinds of questions have different answers in different localities. In some cases, towns right next to each other can handle local elections completely differently. Given the number of local elections around the country, it's hard to say what's most common or what's the best system for any particular area.

The rules for federal and state elections in your state are easy to find online. For local elections, you might visit your town or municipality's website. The public library, city hall, or other local government offices might be your best bet for learning more information about the specific local races in your community. The local newspaper, or a website dedicated to news about the area, will be able to tell you more about who's running and provide some details about their positions.

Now that we've talked about how voting works around the country, we'll take a look at political parties and the role they play in the process. ■

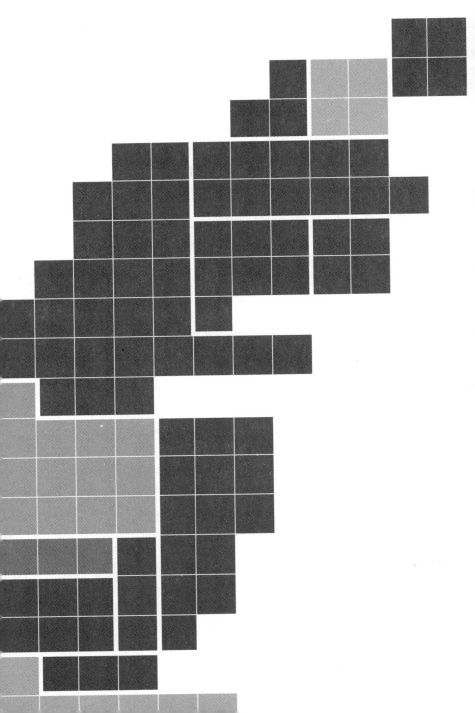

CHAPTER 3

PARTY TIME: THE ROLE OF POLITICAL PARTIES IN US POLITICS

In the first two chapters, we talked a bit about the role of political parties in American elections. The founders didn't design the system of government with parties in mind, and the Constitution doesn't say anything about them, but they've become an important part of governing the country.

Basically, any political party is an organized group of people who share ideas about government policy and work to elect officials who support those policies. Obviously, not everyone in a party or every candidate will agree with the party leadership on every single issue, but the members tend to agree more than they disagree—or at least they agree with one another more than they do with members of rival parties.

You might already have a party preference, but you don't need to have one. Over the past three decades, an increasing number of Americans have chosen to identify as independent (in 2014, according to the polling firm Gallup, that number hit an all-time record of 43 percent). Still, a fair number of self-described independents pick one party's candidates most of the time; they just don't like to think of themselves as party members for whatever reason (a January 2016 Gallup analysis found only about 12 percent of voters were truly independent in their voting patterns). We'll take a quick look at how political parties formed, what they do, and what the major and minor ones mean today.

Section I
Getting Parties Started

The idea of political parties is usually traced to England in the late seventeenth century, when supporters of a constitutional monarchy with a powerful legislature became the Whigs, and supporters of a stronger, absolute monarchy formed the Tories. That's not untrue; the Whig/Tory divide is a good first example of parties in the modern sense. But they grew out of an older idea.

Most governments throughout history didn't need political organizations because there were no elections. People took power through war, marriage, or just being the closest living relative of the last ruler.

However, societies that made use of voting couldn't help but have political factions. For example, ancient Rome had clear political divisions between the powerful and the masses (the patricians and the plebeians, to use the Roman terms). Rome also often saw groups of powerful individuals teaming up to support a certain candidate or to sabotage one. (There would be fewer Shakespeare plays otherwise.) What was different about seventeenth-century England was that the parties were organized around issues instead of just supporting individuals, and they set up a formal way to select candidates for office who would back the party agenda.

These days, political parties are common in every democratic government around the world. That model has been so successful that even dictators often organize their own political parties and hold "elections" they have no chance of losing. Because the United States was founded and led by former British citizens who grew up among Whigs and Tories, and because several of the founders were particularly fascinated by Roman ideas and history, parties were hardly an unfamiliar concept to them.

In his farewell address to the nation in September 1796, President George Washington warned the American people to avoid political parties, which he saw as a way for ambitious people to rise to power without first gaining the support of the governed. That speech gets mentioned a lot by people who don't like the party system, but Washington had the advantage of running more or less unopposed, at a time when most Americans who could vote saw him as the obvious leader for the nation. He also said that more than a century before primaries existed, back when the notion of voters selecting party nominees wasn't even considered a possibility.

The American two-party system we all know (and some people love) has its roots in 1796, when Washington's choice to step down after two terms gave the country its first election between competing political parties.

THE HISTORY OF THE TWO-PARTY SYSTEM

The earliest political parties in the United States formed within Washington's cabinet, during his first term. A series of policies introduced by Secretary of the Treasury Alexander Hamilton—the

Federalists' leading policy wonk—were heavily opposed by Secretary of State Thomas Jefferson, and the differences between those two rivals more or less created the United States' first partisan divide as an independent nation.

The Federalists (Hamilton's folks) wanted a strong central government, an economy focused on commerce and trade, and a close relationship with Great Britain. The Republicans (Jefferson's side) wanted the state governments to have more influence, for the economy to be based on farming and local industries, and for the United States to have stronger ties with France instead of its former home country. (Despite the name it was called at the time, the party was a completely different organization from today's Republican Party, so most historians now call it the Democratic-Republican Party. This book will do that too, starting . . . now.)

Washington still ran for reelection without any serious opposition (even Jefferson wanted him to run again, correctly guessing that he could keep the young country united). When the first president decided not to go for a third term, however, the next election featured a faceoff between two parties. In one corner, the vice president, John Adams, represented the Federalists. In the other, Thomas Jefferson ran as the nominee of the Democratic-Republicans.

Adams won the first round. By finishing second, Jefferson became vice president, thanks to a quirk in the system later eliminated by the Twelfth Amendment (see sidebar on page 102). Four years later, Jefferson won the rematch. For the first time in modern Western history, an opposition party had taken over in a peaceful, democratic election. This Revolution of 1800 is a bigger deal than people might realize. There was a good chance that the system could have failed and the country could have split up; instead, the election proved the American system could work.

This First Party System, which started with the Federalists and the Democratic-Republicans, lasted from about 1792 until 1824. However, that included a few years in which much of the country was down to a one-party system. The Federalists began to fall apart as an organization after the War of 1812 ended, the Democratic-Republicans controlled more than 80 percent of Congress, popular president James Monroe incorporated some of the Federalists' ideas, and national debates briefly stopped being defined by partisan politics. Thanks to its less divided political culture, that stretch became known as the Era of Good Feelings.

Like most good feelings, it didn't last forever. All it took was the chaotic 1824 election of John Quincy Adams to end it (see page 74). The Democratic-Republicans split into two new parties, with Andrew Jackson founding a new Democratic Party and, in 1833, Henry Clay and Daniel Webster starting the opposition Whig Party, naming it after England's old nonconformist faction. Two major parties were again the norm. The Whigs fell apart in 1856, and a new Republican Party (the most successful of several new entities that tried to replace the Whigs) became the second major force in American politics. The Republicans and Democrats have been the dominant institutions ever since.

THE TWO-PARTY SYSTEM TODAY

So that's where they came from, and parties have a lot of say when it comes to both elections and governing in the United States.

A GLITCH IN THE SYSTEM

Originally, because the Constitution provided for a president and a vice president, every elector could pick two candidates. The winner would be president and the second-place finisher vice president. That worked at first, because George Washington was a unanimous selection. In 1792 the Federalists renominated John Adams for vice president, and he kept his job by earning more votes than the Democratic-Republican–backed George Clinton (77–50, while Washington received 132 votes).

In 1796 Adams chose Thomas Pinckney as his preferred vice president, but they still needed to run separately, and Thomas Jefferson's second-place finish in the Electoral College meant he got the job. The 1800 race produced an even stranger result. Jefferson and his vice-presidential choice, Aaron Burr, received equal support in the Electoral College—and because those votes weren't separated by office, they tied for the presidency. The House of Representatives needed to break the tie. Jefferson's longtime rival Alexander Hamilton helped persuade the representatives to choose a man he disagreed with but respected, instead of Burr. To avoid the kind of chaos those two elections produced, in 1803 both houses of Congress passed the Twelfth Amendment, which established that electors should vote separately for president and vice president (the states ratified it before the 1804 election, and Jefferson dropped Burr from the ticket).

Hamilton and Burr clashed several more times. When Burr ran for governor of New York, a newspaper published a letter from Hamilton calling him a "dangerous man" not to be trusted in government. That led to their famous duel, in which Burr shot and killed Hamilton on July 11, 1804.

The 1800 election wasn't the main reason why Alexander Hamilton and Aaron Burr wound up firing guns at each other . . . but it didn't help.

Most democratic governments around the world now have a multiparty political system. In parliamentary systems with a prime minister (the United Kingdom, Australia, Canada, and many others), voters don't directly choose the PM; they vote for their local member of parliament. If the majority of members come from the same party, that party's self-selected leader becomes prime minister. (It's a bit like the way the Speaker of the House is chosen.) If no party has more than 50 percent of the seats, at least two parties, or as many as it takes to hold a majority, need to work out a deal to support one another in a coalition that elects a prime minister. And if the coalition parties stop getting along, one can leave the coalition, cost the prime minister his or her job, and force a new election. Plus, the prime minister's party can replace them at almost any time, so the person voters thought would be in charge won't necessarily serve a whole term.

Here's another example of how the United States government is unusual.

The United States government is technically a multiparty system too. The system wasn't created to benefit only two parties, but a lot of things about the system made it easy for that one-or-the-other system to become normal.

One reason for that is the winner-take-all nature of voting here, especially for the office of president. With the way the Electoral College is set up, an individual candidate needs to win a majority of the national electoral vote, so candidates with the nationwide organization provided by major parties have an advantage. Once the Federalist versus Democratic-Republican split became a dividing line, both sides realized it made more sense to rally behind one candidate who would share their overall platform rather than see a few candidates with their perspective split votes and let the other side win key states. Remember, too, that senators were originally chosen by state legislatures, so you can see how that made it attractive for factions in the legislatures to organize by party. So while a candidate doesn't have to belong to one of the two major parties to win an election, it really helps.

The same thing is true once candidates become legislators at the federal or state level. Which bills Congress and state legislatures bring to the floor is largely up to the party that holds the majority, because it appoints the chairs for committees and elects the majority leader or speaker. It's possible to get elected without being a member of the two big parties, but even the most independent of independents pretty much have to caucus with one party or the other if they're going to have any influence in how laws are passed.

There's definitely a lot of chicken-and-egg thinking in how the two-party system perpetuates itself. The system makes it easier for candidates from one of two major parties to win, and polls show Americans often choose not to vote for other candidates because of a feeling that they can't win, which becomes a self-fulfilling prophecy. Plus, any new laws governing how candidates are chosen are, by definition, going to be written by government officials who already won elections. Nearly all of them are going to be either Democrats or Republicans, and the one thing the leadership of those two parties will always be able to agree on is wanting to keep the two-party system around.

DRAWING THE DISTRICTS

One of the common complaints about voting is that the American people hate Congress but are big fans of their own congressional representatives. Results show that this conventional wisdom is true, and it's a good example of why the two-party system is hard to replace.

The 2014 midterm elections were a particularly extreme example. The Republican-controlled House had extremely low approval ratings. Less than a month before Election Day, polls by CNN, Fox, CBS, ABC, and NBC found an average of only 14 percent of Americans approved of the job Congress was doing. (That was better than the record-low 9 percent approval the same Congress had in 2012, but not by much.) There are diseases with approval ratings not that much lower. You might think that would cost many congresspeople their jobs . . . but you would be wrong. More than 96 percent of incumbent members of the House kept their jobs, and the party in power actually *gained* thirteen seats in the House. Two years later, the average margin of victory for a successful House candidate was about 37 percent, and forty-two states had no seriously competitive House race.

One big reason for that is the process of redistricting, when state legislatures redraw their federal House districts every ten years to reflect the results of the national census. Other than the states that have only one representative (as of 2020, seven out of fifty), the others have to redraw House districts to reflect changes to the state's population.

The catch is that census results only tell them how many House districts the state will have, and federal law only requires that the districts have roughly the same number of voters. Beyond that, states get to play by their own rules, and how they divide those voters into districts can have decade-long effects on who the states send to Congress.

GERRY'S "MANDER"

The term *gerrymander* dates back to 1812, when Massachusetts redrew its state legislative districts with some bizarre shapes rather than traditional squares and rectangles. The state's governor, Elbridge Gerry, signed a law that allowed the unconventional redistricting, which drew the map so that Gerry's Democratic-Republican supporters would have an advantage.

A *Boston Gazette* political cartoon in March of that year turned the odd shape of the new districts into a snakelike monster and called it a *Gerry-mander* (as in, the governor's name mashed up with a salamander). Federalists unhappy with Gerry's strategy made sure the insult stuck, but the new boundary lines secured Democratic-Republican control of the state senate. Gerry's unpopular move made it harder to save his own job, though; he lost the governorship to a Federalist.

The cartoon version of Gerry's map may look ridiculous, but it's nothing compared to some of today's partisan maps.

Six states—California, Washington, Arizona, Idaho, and (if they ever get enough people for districts to matter) Alaska and Montana—have independent commissions in charge of redistricting. These commissions don't include elected officials, and they try to draw the districts in a nonpartisan way. In thirty-seven states, on the other hand, the legislatures get to design districts, and they usually do it a very partisan way. This kind of redistricting is also called *gerrymandering* (see sidebar on page 107). In theory, you could live in the same house your entire life and change congressional districts every ten years, just because your state legislators see that change as an advantage. Take a look at a map of most large states' congressional districts, and you'll see the weird, amoeba-like shapes legislators design to put voters where they want them.

What that means is the party that controls the state legislature gets to decide which voters live in which districts, and that often means arranging voters so that the party doing the deciding has advantages in as many districts as possible. That can mean grouping large numbers of the other side's voters into a small number of districts, letting them have a few "safe" seats but giving them less of a chance anywhere else. Or it could involve distributing areas with lots of opposition voters so widely that the opposition will have a hard time winning any seats. The approach depends on the state's demographics. Sometimes the shape of the redraw is specifically designed so that two popular incumbents of the same party wind up in the same district and have to run against each other, knocking one out of Congress. Other times, in states that require officials to live in the district they represent (which not all states do), it can mean redrawing boundaries so that an incumbent congressperson winds up living outside of that district and becoming ineligible for a job they already have.

At times, gerrymandering has been used for more idealistic purposes. In the South after the Civil War, it was sometimes used to draw districts where former slaves would have enough numbers to be a factor. These days, though, it's usually done for short-term political gain. And because the districts might be redrawn once a decade, who you elect to your state legislature can be particularly important when their term will overlap with the next round of redistricting. That's particularly important in 2020, because there will also be a new national census.

Partisan redistricting happens because it works for the party in charge. Lately, it's been a big help to Republicans. In 2012 Democratic candidates for the House of Representatives received more than 1.5 million more votes combined than did all of the Republican candidates nationwide, but the GOP still won 234 out of 435 seats for a clear majority in the House. In 2016 Republicans won the House 241–194 but received less than 50 percent of the total vote nationwide. Two years later, Democrats gained 40 seats to retake the House, but that required breaking the midterm record for the biggest cumulative margin of victory nationwide.

It kind of stinks if you live in a district drawn so that candidates you support have little to no chance, as who represents you in Washington can impact what federal services or programs your hometown receives. It also makes it easier for candidates with extreme views to get elected in some places, because when the district is designed so they can't lose, they don't have to worry about appealing to voters who aren't already on their side. That's an underrated factor in the hyper-partisanship of current national politics.

The most extreme recent example of partisan gerrymandering happened in Texas in 2003. That was the first time Republicans had controlled both houses of the Texas state legislature in more than a century (since before the Civil War), and they made the controversial decision to change the districts in the middle of the decade rather than waiting for the next census like everybody else. Democratic legislators didn't have the numbers to stop them, and those legislators actually fled the state temporarily to make sure the legislature couldn't have enough members present for a quorum (and, by leaving Texas, to make sure state law enforcement couldn't force them to go back). A lawsuit over the controversy went to the Supreme Court, which ruled in favor of the states being able to redistrict more than once a decade, setting a potentially dangerous precedent. (It also ruled that one of the redrawn districts was a violation of the 1965 Civil Rights Act and ordered it redrawn.)

So not only do voters pick which party has power in the state legislature, but the party in power often gets to pick its voters. Like the Electoral College, gerrymandering makes the country less democratic than it would be otherwise. But also like the Electoral College, it is now so entrenched that it would be awfully hard to eliminate.

THE PROS AND CONS

From a voter perspective, candidates having a party affiliation isn't without its benefits. For one thing, it usually offers some sense of where a candidate is going to stand on certain issues. Elsewhere in this book, there are tips for how to become an informed voter, but the sad reality is that the country will also always have millions of uninformed voters. For them, party affiliation is an easy way to decide which candidate is more likely to share their politics. (Which, again, is why trying to pick each party's best candidate in a primary can be so important.)

For a candidate, having the backing of a party organization can be a huge help. Party leadership will almost always support its incumbents in a primary (unless the incumbent did something to really tick off the party). But whether incumbents win or lose, the party will usually give its support to whoever wins the nomination. For candidates, that means the party is a source of money, logistical support, help with getting out the vote, you name it. Candidates running in a down-ballot race—for a seat in the state senate or to be county sheriff, for instance—can get a boost from voter turnout for the party's other candidates. If, say, the state Republican Party has a popular candidate running for governor, the coattails effect helps other Republicans on the same ballot. Parties also play a role in developing political careers. A candidate or elected official who makes a name for himself or herself might be groomed for higher office by the local or state party. From a getting-things-done perspective, parties can help turn bills into laws, as the representative introducing legislation has team members with an interest in getting that legislation passed.

On the other hand, there's a case to be made that a two-party system makes the country slower to change, particularly on those issues where the two major parties generally agree with how things currently stand. For example, at the federal level, the majority of both parties' representatives consistently support increasing the military budget, oppose most gun control, and support tariff-free trade deals (which allow companies to import cheap goods for

American consumers but also make it easier for companies to send American jobs overseas). While the two parties debate certain topics vigorously, debates on issues like these are often a matter of arguing about details or about matters of degree.

At the same time, this system often turns politics into a team sport, with people just supporting whatever their preferred party does and complaining about whatever the other party does. That's become worse too. It's hard to pinpoint exactly when things became more partisan, but many historians date it to the 1980 election, and there are a number of reasons why the last few decades have seen the divide deepen—from the rise of hyper-partisan news networks such as Fox News and Breitbart, to the spread of misinformation online and on social media, to the increased use of undemocratic tactics including the filibuster and gerrymandering, to the ever-bigger role of donor money in politics, to demographic changes in several states.

All these things make it harder to pass laws because they can make politics more about defeating the other side than about governing the country. After the passage of the Affordable Care Act, the healthcare law that was one of President Barack Obama's biggest legislative victories, the Republican majority in the House of Representatives held more than fifty separate votes to repeal the law, even though everyone knew the Senate and President Obama weren't going to get rid of it, making the constant votes a pointless political exercise and (as even quite a few Republicans tried to point out) a waste of time and energy. That's a new level of obstructionism, and it's a symptom of that unfortunate team-sport approach to politics.

Of course, it doesn't need to be that way. Parties have always had disagreements on lots of subjects, but they didn't always automatically oppose each other. Not that long ago, many issues that are now partisan had broad bipartisan support, including major programs.

Many of the environmental protections that came about in the 1970s, such as the formation of the Environmental Protection Agency and the passing of the Clean Air Act and Clean Water Act, were supported by the Democratic-controlled Congress and signed by Republican president Richard Nixon. The majority of both parties' congressional contingents voted in support of Democratic president Franklin Roosevelt's plan to create Social Security; that retirement fund is now an institution and one of America's most popular government programs. Longtime senators Bob Dole and George McGovern, seen respectively as a very conservative Republican and a very liberal Democrat in their time, worked together to create the modern food stamp program to help poor Americans feed their families. This isn't ancient history, and not every issue needs to have a partisan divide.

Section II
The Major Parties

The Democratic Party is generally considered the mainstream liberal party in American politics, and the Republican Party is the mainstream conservative party. That hasn't always been the case, as we've seen, but it shows no sign of changing anytime soon.

The Democratic Party is one of the oldest political parties anywhere in the world, and that means it has had plenty of time to change along with the country. The early version that formed by supporters of Andrew Jackson was most popular in the South, focused largely on the needs of farmers, and opposed the creation of a central bank. The Republican Party that ran Abraham Lincoln for president in 1860 formed in opposition to the spread of slavery and was a mostly northern party. Suffice it to say, those descriptions have become pretty outdated.

The modern differences between the two parties, and how they have evolved over time, could easily be a whole book (or, honestly, a series of long books). So describing the differences requires huge oversimplifications, but here goes. In general, the modern national Republican Party tends to support business interests when it comes to economic issues, a more militarily focused foreign policy, and more government intervention in social issues. In contrast, the national Democratic Party tends to support middle-class and working-class interests in terms of economic issues, a more diplomatically focused foreign policy, and less government intervention in social issues.

By the middle of the twentieth century, the Democrats had become associated with large-scale government programs, as President Franklin Roosevelt and Congress passed the New Deal, a series of reforms aimed at helping the country recover from the Great Depression. These included programs such as infrastructure jobs for unemployed workers, the Social Security retirement program, and regulations on banks and security traders. Future Democratic administrations introduced more reforms, including the healthcare programs Medicare and Medicaid, often as part of similar initiatives with names like the Fair Deal or Great Society. The Democrats were the dominant party until the party split over civil rights laws, especially during the 1960s, losing much of its southern support when national Democrats took the lead in passing laws to fight discrimination against African Americans. The party is still associated with government-based solutions to society's problems.

The Republican Party also evolved during the last century. While many Republicans supported New Deal-style policies at the time, by the 1960s the party saw a split between its old-school, pro-business establishment and new *movement conservatives*, who opposed large government programs (other than a bigger military) and wanted their conservative interpretation of Christian values to be a bigger factor in how the government approached social issues. The 1980 election of Ronald Reagan is often seen as the point when movement conservatives became the main force in the GOP, and they generally moved the party in a more conservative direction. The Democratic Party during the same span has also shifted to the right (obviously, not nearly as much), so that current Democratic policies sometimes seem like Republican policies from a generation ago.

Here's a quick (and, once again, very incomplete) breakdown of how modern Democrats and Republicans approach issues.

On economic issues, for example, members of both parties talk about wanting to pay the country's bills by cutting taxes and reducing spending, but the specifics of their solutions are usually different. More often than not, Republicans talk about wanting to cut federal income taxes, while Democrats usually propose a more progressive income tax rate (meaning the people in the highest income bracket pay a higher percentage of their income in taxes). As an example of how things change in politics, the top marginal

"The Democrats are the party that says government will make you smarter, taller, richer, and remove the crabgrass on your lawn. Republicans are the party that says government doesn't work, and then they get elected and prove it."

—P. J. O'ROURKE, COMEDIAN, AUTHOR, AND LONGTIME REPUBLICAN

tax rate—the highest percentage anyone pays in federal income taxes, and which only applies to earnings above certain dollar amounts—was 92 percent in 1953, during Dwight Eisenhower's presidency. After several decreases, it hit a recent low of 28 percent in 1988, and is 37 percent as of 2019. On the spending side, Republicans usually vote to increase the military budget, where the majority of the country's discretionary spending already goes, while voting to cut other government programs rather than raise taxes. Democrats, meanwhile, are more likely to talk about increasing spending (or at least not cutting spending) on social programs such as education and healthcare, rather than focusing on tax cuts.

If we're being honest, the country usually spends much more money than it generates in taxes and other revenue, and that's probably going to be true for the foreseeable future. Both parties have overseen large increases in spending; the difference is what they prioritize with their spending and how much of it is covered by taxes.

Something similar is true for when the parties support government regulation. Many social conservatives in the Republican

Party want the government to make rules banning abortion or marriage between gay and lesbian couples, while Democrats are more likely to want the government staying out of those decisions. On the other hand, many Republicans will argue for the business community rather than the government deciding what to do about issues such as the environment or healthcare, while Democrats support more federal regulation in those areas. The Articles of Confederation proved the United States wouldn't succeed with a small government, but parties have never stopped arguing over exactly where the government's influence should be big or small.

WHO SUPPORTS WHOM

Again, this can't help but be an oversimplification, but there are trends in terms of where the parties get their support. These days, based on polling data and election results, the Democratic Party is strongest in the Northeast, the upper Midwest, the West Coast, and parts of the Mountain West, while the Republican Party is strongest in the South, the lower Midwest, and parts of the West. Democrats fare better in cities and Republicans in rural areas and smaller towns, with suburbs somewhere in the middle.

There are also noticeable patterns as far as who votes for which party. Between 1980 and 2016, the Republican presidential nominee has performed better with men than with women in every election, while the Democratic nominee has done the opposite. Over that same period, white voters chose the Republican in most cases (the exception was 1996, when Bill Clinton received 46 percent of the white vote to Bob Dole's 45), while voters of color overwhelmingly favored Democrats (African

WAVES OF POWER

Political parties tend to take turns holding federal power for long stretches, and that includes the presidency. Some of that is a natural ebb and flow between two parties, some is because the parties' positions evolve, and some has to do with changing voter demographics.

Here's how the presidents have broken down by party:

- Republicans (19): Abraham Lincoln,* Ulysses Grant, Rutherford Hayes, James Garfield, Chester Arthur, Benjamin Harrison, William McKinley, Theodore Roosevelt, William Howard Taft, Warren Harding, Calvin Coolidge, Herbert Hoover, Dwight Eisenhower, Richard Nixon, Gerald Ford, Ronald Reagan, George H. W. Bush, George W. Bush, Donald Trump
- Democrats (15**): Andrew Jackson, Martin Van Buren, James Polk, Franklin Pierce, James Buchanan, Andrew Johnson,* Grover Cleveland, Woodrow Wilson, Franklin Roosevelt, Harry Truman, John Kennedy, Lyndon Johnson, Jimmy Carter, Bill Clinton, Barack Obama

American voters by the largest margin, including a historic 99–1 margin in support of Barack Obama in 2008). Which party different demographic groups back is both a cause and an effect of policy. Voters support parties they see as having their interests in mind, and parties back policies that are popular with their supporters and will inspire those supporters to volunteer, campaign, and vote.

Every four years, as part of the national conventions that offi-

- Democratic-Republicans (4): Thomas Jefferson, James Madison, James Monroe, John Quincy Adams
- Whigs (4): William Henry Harrison, John Tyler, Zachary Taylor, Millard Fillmore
- Federalists (1): John Adams
- No Party (1): George Washington***

*Both Lincoln and Andrew Johnson served as president as members of the National Union Party, which was the name their ticket used in 1864 as a show of Union solidarity during the Civil War. However, that was more of a campaign tactic than any kind of organized party.

**The Democrats' number is a little lower but includes the only president to serve nonconsecutive terms (Cleveland was both the twenty-second and twenty-fourth president), and the only one to serve more than two terms (Franklin Roosevelt, elected four times and president for a record twelve years and change).

***We covered this earlier.

cially nominate the presidential and vice-presidential candidates, the parties adopt a *platform*—a formal document that explains where the party officially stands on various issues. The platform isn't binding; individual candidates don't have to adopt all, or even any, of it. Still, it's a good way to see what the party leadership and the presidential nominee want to do for (or, depending on your perspective, to) the country.

You can find the most recent Democratic and Republican

platforms on the parties' official websites, and reading through older versions is a good way to understand how the parties, and American politics in general, have evolved. Not only can you see how the parties' positions on various issues have changed, but you can also see what issues were considered important enough nationally for the parties to feel the need to take an official position.

When we talk about party stances on issues here, it's important to point out that this primarily means the national party. Each state has its own Democratic Party and Republican Party, which obviously coordinate with their national counterparts and state-level candidates. As we discussed earlier, the United States has always had serious regional differences, and parties need to run candidates who can win in their home states. Therefore, while many national Democrats oppose oil drilling in Alaska, the party's candidates there usually support it, in part because many voters there are employed by the extraction industry. Both parties often run candidates in the South who are more socially conservative than the same parties' candidates in New England. And so on.

The interaction between national and state parties can be quirky. As we discussed back in chapter 2, voters sometimes split their tickets, voting for different parties at the federal and state levels. Also, remember that federal congressional districts in a majority of states are decided by state legislatures, while national parties dictate the states' primary schedule (except in cases like the Michigan example on page 79, when states defy the national party).

At the local level, parties might or might not be as important, depending on where you live. Your local mayor might run as part of a party ticket, or he or she might appear on the ballot without any party affiliation. In New York City, it's not unusual for mayors to run on the tickets of smaller parties as well as their main one. Chicago used to have primaries for mayor, but they were a formality in such a heavily Democratic city. It now has a nonpartisan February election that pits all candidates against one another, with a runoff between the top two finishers if nobody gets at least 50 percent. Some states have state parties, county parties, and local or municipal parties, all of which might work together or might get territorial.

In some cases, candidates running for local offices will form their own local tickets, meaning candidates for the city council and other boards endorse one another and campaign together, but voters can still pick members of other tickets. Those tickets can be part of a major party, or they can just be their own thing with their own name. Local parties might exist for just one election cycle, or they can last as long as their candidates' entire careers.

One of the more troubling trends in politics is the number of candidates running unopposed, particularly in areas where, thanks to factors including gerrymandering, one party thinks it has little to no chance of electing someone and just gives up. In 2014, for example, thirty-one members of the House of Representatives—sixteen Republicans and fifteen Democrats—ran without serious opposition in the general election. That included six seats in Massachusetts alone, and five in Florida. Driven by Donald Trump's historic unpopularity, Democrats contested all but one House seat in 2018, though that doesn't mean the trend is over, and seventeen Democratic seats went unopposed. Those are examples where two huge national parties have an interest in going after the job. In 2016, 42 percent of races for seats in state legislatures featured no major-party opposition. In a smaller town, you might have a mayor who's been mayor forever or a member of the city council who never draws a real challenge from anybody.

That's a situation where independents and third parties can be helpful, and we'll talk about them next.

Section III
Third Parties

Third party has become a catchall term for anyone running for office who isn't representing one of the two major parties. At any given moment, there might be an eighth or ninth or forty-first party, but they're all still talked about as third parties.

Because the term third party is so broad, it covers a wide variety of candidates. A third-party candidacy could mean a former president like Teddy Roosevelt trying to get his old job back (see sidebar on page 126). Or it could mean a celebrity running as a gag, as comedian Will Rogers did in 1928 or fellow comedian Gracie Allen did in 1940. Or it could be a one-issue candidate trying to get alcohol eliminated or convince the country to base the value of money on the price of silver. Or it could mean anything in between.

There are two main categories of third-party candidates. One is candidates who run without a party affiliation at all, as independents. The other is candidates who run on the ticket of an organized party other than the Democrats or Republicans.

To win as a true independent at the national or state level, a candidate usually needs some built-in name recognition, because they won't have an existing organization to help them get on the

BEST OF BOTH WORLDS

Every so often, the country's leading historians are polled and asked to rank the best (and worst) presidents in order. The ranking of the top five changes, but the names in those top spots have usually remained the same in survey after survey. In chronological order, that list is George Washington, Thomas Jefferson, Abraham Lincoln, Theodore Roosevelt, and Franklin Roosevelt.

Not surprisingly, that includes the four faces on Mount Rushmore (Franklin Roosevelt hadn't yet been elected when that monument was created) and all the presidents with monuments on the National Mall in Washington, DC (which swaps one Roosevelt for the other). That top-five list also includes a range of political parties, with two Republicans, one Democrat, one Democratic-Republican, and the party-less Washington.

As long as we're on the subject, a 2015 *Washington Post* survey of leading historians graded each president's performance on a 1-to-100 scale, and the results were pretty strong. Twenty-four out of forty-three presidents scored at least fifty out of one hundred, with Lincoln and Washington above ninety.

ballot, raise money, set up campaign events, or get voters to the polls on Election Day. On the other hand, organized third parties might have some experience with those aspects of a campaign and boast a certain number of already committed voters, but they also might have a track record of losing that a well-known independent could be better off without. It all depends on the candidate, the party, and the specifics of the race.

WINNING SOLO

If we're being honest, one of the biggest mistakes modern third parties make is focusing way too heavily on the presidential election, rather than electing viable candidates to smaller offices and building from the ground up. Still, even with all the power the two parties hold, candidates from outside them sometimes win important elections. We'll look at a few recent examples.

In 1990 Bernie Sanders of Vermont became the first independent elected to the House of Representatives in forty years, and he was reelected seven times to his seat as Vermont's only congressperson. In 2006 he ran for the Senate instead, won with more than 65 percent of the vote, and won his 2012 and 2018 reelections by even bigger margins. He's a good example of the independent approach and holds the record as the longest-serving independent in Congress.

Angus King is another good example. In Maine, voters chose the independent King as governor in 1994 and reelected him in 1998. Maine limits its governors to two terms, but after a few years away from government, King ran for the Senate in 2012 and was elected with almost 53 percent of the vote.

As for the existing-party approach, in 1998 Jesse Ventura—a former small-town mayor better known for his long career as a professional wrestler and star of action movies such as *Predator*—was elected governor of Minnesota as the candidate of the Reform Party, which had been founded a few years earlier by presidential candidate Ross Perot. Ventura not only won but also defeated two well-known major-party opponents. When Senator Paul Wellstone died (see page 84), Ventura needed to appoint a temporary senator to serve the end of Wellstone's term and picked Dean Barkley.

Barkley, who was a founder of the Minnesota Reform Party and had previously run an unsuccessful House race as that party's nominee, spent two months as an independent United States senator. However, one thing Democratic and Republican legislators in Minnesota agreed on was wanting Ventura out, so the governor often had a tough time getting the legislature to work with him and chose not to run for a second term.

Other officials were originally affiliated with one of the major parties, then switched parties or ran as independents because of disagreements with their former colleagues.

Bob Smith, a Republican senator from New Hampshire, left the party in 2000 after failing to gain much traction in the presidential primaries and stayed in the Senate as an independent. In 2001 senator Jim Jeffords of Vermont left the Republican Party, became an independent, and chose to caucus with the Democrats instead of his old party. The Senate was divided fifty-fifty at the time, so Jeffords' shift changed which party controlled the chamber (and got him kicked out of an all-Republican-senator barbershop quartet).

Joe Lieberman of Connecticut, the Democratic vice-presidential nominee in 2000, alienated many of his supporters by backing the invasion of Iraq and lost the 2006 primary for his Senate seat. However, he then ran as a third-party independent and kept his seat by defeating the man who'd beaten him a few months earlier. Lincoln Chafee, a Republican senator from Rhode Island and the son of another longtime Rhode Island senator, split with the party over the Iraq invasion and refused to vote for President George W. Bush in 2004. After losing to a Democrat in his 2006 reelection bid, Chafee became an independent and in 2010 was elected governor of his state without a party affiliation.

TRYING A REPEAT PERFORMANCE

Not all candidates running as third-party nominees are outsider long shots. Three times in history, a former president ran for his old job without the support of either major party, though none pulled off a victory.

MARTIN VAN BUREN (1848) After one term as vice president to Andrew Jackson and one term as president, Van Buren lost his reelection race in 1840 and tried unsuccessfully to become the Democratic nominee again in 1844.

Four years later, slavery was finally becoming more of an electoral issue. A new political party, the Free Soil Party, saw Van Buren as a big enough name to earn the party some national attention, and his antislavery views were a natural fit. He received more than 10 percent of the national popular vote in November but didn't win any electoral votes. Still, he finished second in his home state of New York, ahead of Democratic nominee Lewis Cass—guaranteeing Whig Zachary Taylor the state's electoral votes, which were enough for Taylor to win the presidency instead of Cass.

MILLARD FILLMORE (1856) Fillmore was never elected president. He was vice president when Taylor died in office in 1850 and served more than two years in the White House. Enough members of the Whig Party were unhappy with his performance—especially his signing of the Fugitive Slave Act, which made it easier to return runaway slaves to the South and punished anyone who helped them—that the party chose to run General Winfield Scott in 1852 instead of the incumbent Fillmore.

By 1856, the Whigs were no more, with the new Republican Party and others trying to win over their voters. Fillmore became the nominee of the American Party, a nativist party that opposed immigration (it was especially anti-Catholic and therefore against any immigration from Italy or Ireland). Better known as the "Know Nothing" party because of its secret origins, the party had elected a number of mayors in major cities (including Boston, Philadelphia, and Washington, DC) in 1854. Fillmore hadn't been a party member and didn't share some of its more extreme views, but Know Nothing leaders thought he would appeal to enough former Whigs to compete for the presidency. They knew nothing. Fillmore won more than 21 percent of the popular vote, but only Maryland's eight electoral votes.

THEODORE ROOSEVELT (1912) One of the most popular and influential presidents in history, Roosevelt was disappointed enough with his Republican successor, William Howard Taft, that he decided to run against his former friend for the party's nomination. Roosevelt won primaries in nine of twelve states, with Taft barely winning one, but primaries were still a new thing, and only a few convention delegates were chosen by them.

When the Republican convention stuck with Taft, Roosevelt started his own party, the Progressive Party, which had a convention and nominated candidates for other offices besides president. The party was soon nicknamed the Bull Moose Party (after Roosevelt described himself as feeling "as strong as a bull moose" during his 1912 campaign announcement), and Roosevelt had a pretty strong showing. He actually finished second in the presidential election to Woodrow Wilson, winning more than 27 percent of the vote, and six states totaling eighty-eight electoral votes. (Taft won only about 23 percent and just eight electoral votes, while about 7.5 percent of the popular vote was split between three *other* third parties.)

Candidates such as Lieberman and Chafee already had name recognition in their states, and people there were already used to supporting them, so the known commodities were able to run and win without a party.

On the other hand, as we discussed earlier, the Electoral College—combined with the way the two-party system has developed over time, making it hard for other candidates to get on the ballot or qualify for presidential debates—makes it almost impossible for candidates from third parties to win the presidency. It's one reason why Bernie Sanders, who never previously identified as a Democrat during a long political career (he first ran for office in 1972 and was elected mayor of Burlington, Vermont, in 1981) announced in May of 2015 that he would seek the Democratic Party's 2016 nomination for president rather than try to run a third-party presidential campaign. (Less than a month later, Lincoln Chafee also announced he would seek the Democratic nomination, though he dropped out of the race in October, well before the Iowa caucuses.) Sanders finished a strong second to Hillary Clinton, winning twenty-two primaries or caucuses and 46 percent of pledged delegates to the convention. In April 2017, a Harvard-Harris poll found his campaign had made Sanders the active US politician with the highest approval rating among registered voters (57 percent), though it was still lower than former president Obama's.

THE OTHER GUYS

For candidates who want to run with a third party that already exists, American politics offers many more options than you might think.

Throughout history, there have often been one-issue parties, in which individual candidates might have differences on other issues, but all run mostly to push one specific policy point. The Free Soil Party of the 1840s (see sidebar on page 126) is a good example, running specifically to stop slavery from spreading to any new states. The Prohibition Party, started in 1869, was a major force in making a ban on alcohol a national issue. Both the Free Soil and Prohibition Parties serve as pretty good examples for how third parties can introduce an issue into the national debate (or make an issue a bigger deal), only to see one or both of the major parties feel like they need to adopt the cause. These parties can play a role in changing policy, for better or worse, and sometimes that's easier than electing candidates.

One-issue parties still exist. The Alaskan Independence Party is the third-largest party in Alaska, with more than ten thousand registered voters. It started as a petition drive, focused on the idea that Alaskans should have had a 1958 vote on whether to remain a territory, become a state, or become a country (and the party supported a referendum to make that vote happen). By 1984, that petition drive had turned into a registered political party. In 1990 ex-Republican Walter Hickel won the governor job on the AIP ticket . . . but then opposed a vote for that referendum and switched back to the GOP late in his term.

Other parties have run on a national platform, specifically trying to nominate a president and build a party. The Socialist Party of America ran candidates for president in quite a few elections, including nominating union leader Eugene V. Debs five times, with a labor-focused, left-of-center platform. The Reform Party, mentioned earlier, ran candidates in the late 1990s on a platform that focused on reducing the national debt.

BEST OF THE REST

In the twentieth century (and early in this one) a handful of third-party candidates managed to top one million votes in a presidential election, and a few even won electoral votes. Unfortunately, Strom Thurmond and George Wallace demonstrated that racists were a large voting bloc, as they specifically campaigned against civil rights for African Americans. Other candidates had nobler platforms, appealing to certain wings of a major party or running to address issues they felt the major parties weren't addressing.

CANDIDATE	PARTY	YEAR	POPULAR VOTE	ELECTORAL VOTE
Theodore Roosevelt	Progressive*	1912	4.1 million (27.4%)	88
Robert LaFollette	Progressive*	1924	4.8 million (16.6%)	13
Strom Thurmond	Dixiecrat	1948	1.2 million (2.4%)	39
Henry Wallace	Progressive*	1948	1.2 million (2.4%)	0
George Wallace	American Independent	1968	9.9 million (12.9%)	46
John Schmitz	American Independent	1972	1.1 million (1.4%)	0
John Anderson	Independent (None)	1980	5.7 million (6.6%)	0
Ross Perot	Independent (None)	1992	19.7 million (18.9%)	0
Ross Perot	Reform	1996	8.1 million (8.4%)	0
Ralph Nader	Green	2000	2.9 million (2.7%)	0
Gary Johnson	Libertarian	2012	1.3 million (1%)	0
Gary Johnson	Libertarian	2016	4.5 million (3.3%)	0
Jill Stein	Green	2016	1.5 million (1%)	0

*Just as there have been multiple Republican Parties, these were different Progressive Parties that shared the same name.

The Progressive Party of the early 1900s supported a wide variety of good-government reforms. In 1948, when President Harry Truman's popularity was at a low point, he had to face two former Democrats running as third-party candidates, with former vice president Henry Wallace on his left and Senator Strom Thurmond on his right (plus Republican Thomas Dewey, who made the election so close that the *Chicago Tribune* famously printed the wrong result).

There are still dozens of small parties out there, from the American Populist Party to the Unity Party of America to the Modern Whig Party to the Socialist Action Party. Most are extremely small, and they aren't helped by the fact that they're often competing with one another for a relatively small number of voters.

Nationally, three parties other than the Republicans and Democrats have more than seventy-five thousand registered voters, so they're worth briefly mentioning: the Libertarian Party, the Green Party, and the Constitution Party.

Founded in 1971, the Libertarian Party focuses on limiting government regulations in terms of both economic and social issues. It usually manages to gain ballot access in presidential elections— its candidates appeared on forty-eight state ballots in 2012 and on all fifty plus Washington, DC, in 2016—but only twice has a Libertarian candidate received one million votes in a presidential election (see chart on page 130). The Green Party, a grassroots party featuring candidates who support preserving the environment, has run presidential candidates since 1996. In 2000 legendary consumer activist Ralph Nader won more than 2.8 million votes and 2.7 percent of the presidential tally in his second campaign as the Green nominee. The Constitution Party, formerly called the US Taxpayers Party, runs to the right of the Republican Party but has never approached the vote totals of even the Libertarians or Greens.

Your state might or might not require you to pick a party when you vote in a primary. For the general election, you can always vote for anyone on the ballot, from any party. And if you ever want to run for office (more on that in chapter 6), you can run with a major or minor party or as an independent. Either way, check out party platforms—they are a good way to see how parties want you to view them, and every candidate will have his or her own policy positions publicized. Doing this research is part of being a good voter, and we'll talk more about that in the next chapter. ■

CHAPTER 4

VOTING (WITH CONFIDENCE)

By now you know a bit more about the United States government, the parties and officials who represent it, and the process for how elections work. The next step is to actually take part in those elections, starting with registering to vote, learning about who and what you can vote for or against, and then actually getting out and doing it.

Section I
Voter Registration

If you're a natural-born citizen of the United States, you automatically become eligible to vote on your eighteenth birthday. If you move here and become a naturalized citizen, you are eligible as soon as that citizenship becomes official, as long as you are eighteen or older. Some states even let you vote earlier than your birthday (in a primary, for example), as long as you'll be eighteen by Election Day in November.

Simply being eligible, though; doesn't mean you can automatically vote. You still need to register. Because states control voting, the procedure can be a little different depending on where you live.

North Dakota is the only state where you don't always need to register. The state got rid of required registration in 1951, but

"Nobody will ever deprive the American people of the right to vote except the American people themselves, and the only way they could do this is by not voting."

—PRESIDENT FRANKLIN ROOSEVELT, IN A 1944 RADIO ADDRESS A FEW WEEKS BEFORE ELECTION DAY (DURING HIS THIRD AND FINAL REELECTION CAMPAIGN)

voters still have to bring an ID and sign in at their local precinct on Election Day. And even in North Dakota, some parts of the state require registration, while others don't.

States also have completely different rules about how early you need to register if you want to take part in an election. In Arkansas, you must register either in person or by mail, and you need to do it thirty days before the election. California requires registration only fifteen days before the election, and you can also take care of it online.

Other states give you more options. In Montana, your registration needs to be postmarked thirty days before the election, but you also have the option of going in person to the county clerk's office (but not a polling place) to register, which you can do all the way up until Election Day. In Colorado, you can register in person on Election Day or save time by completing the process online or by mail at least eight days ahead of time. In Iowa, you can mail your registration if it's postmarked fifteen days before the election, register online or in person ten days before, or register in person on Election Day if you miss those deadlines. Delaware has different rules for general elections and primaries (twenty-four days before the election) versus a special election (ten days before), and voters apply in person, by mail, or online.

State rules change, so make sure to research any updates in yours (everything listed above was true in early 2019 but could change before the 2020 election). The federal government's web portal, USA.gov, gives you an easy way to figure out what you need to register, with links for voters in every state or territory and resources to find your local election office. The many organizations that try to get young voters involved have sites full of resources about where and how to get on the voter rolls (RocktheVote.com and Vote.org are particularly good examples).

The internet's made the whole voting process easier than it was just a generation ago, when you had to sign up in person (possibly while walking uphill both ways in the snow). The majority of states—thirty-eight of them, plus Washington, DC, as of 2019—now allow you to register online, and that number's only going to go up.

MORE WAYS TO REGISTER

In every election cycle, you'll find volunteers with clipboards hanging around in public places, signing people up to register. It's also a useful and easy volunteer opportunity, if you're looking for a way to help people get involved. Volunteers usually set up in spots with heavy foot traffic, like in front of a grocery store or shopping mall, near bus and train stations, at schools, or at big public events. Any number of organizations take part in this kind of registration drive, from political parties and candidates' campaigns to nonpartisan pro-democracy groups such as the League of Women Voters or Rock the Vote.

SCARE TACTICS

You might think getting more Americans involved in their government would be something everyone could agree with. However, in 2008, the Fox News channel and a few other conservative news outlets regularly reported on a "scandal" in which the volunteer organization ACORN turned in registration sheets that included names such as "Mickey Mouse" and "Mary Poppins." Even at the time, this was clearly a misleading story, but Fox continued to report it and some voters believed it was a problem (either for partisan reasons—the group registered more than one million voters, many in heavily Democratic neighborhoods—or just because they didn't understand how the process works).

In case another fake scandal like this comes up again, don't fall for it.

Here's the thing. When you sign up at a voter registration drive, you can put down whatever name and information you want, and the volunteers are required to turn it in with the others. They're not allowed to go through and cross out any of the names on the list, even if some of those names are obviously fake. (They can, and in this case did, flag anyone on the list whose information can't be verified.) The registration forms are turned in to whichever state office handles voting, and officials there need to confirm or deny the registrations.

Even in the extremely unlikely event that state officials treat Mickey Mouse at 123 Fake Street as a real person and register him, he would still have to show up to vote and, per federal rules for a first-time voter, bring either a valid ID or some other proof of address.

If a campaign or party is behind a voting drive, their volunteers aren't allowed to register only supporters of that party, though they understandably might hold their drives in areas where they think their candidate might be popular with newly registered voters. Some states make you register as a member of a party; others let you register without one, and you might or might not ever need to pick a party.

Just because you've registered once doesn't mean you're set and never need to do it again. If you moved your permanent address, even to a different home in the same town, you'll have to re-register. Same thing if you changed your name. If you've moved temporarily—say, if you're away at college or graduate school, in the military, or on a temporary work assignment for a few months—you have a choice. You could change your permanent address to your temporary home and register there, or you could keep your voter registration with the address where you normally live. In that case, you can request an absentee ballot, a process that (as you're probably used to hearing by now) is different from state to state. States also have different rules about how long your voter registration remains valid if you don't use it; miss enough elections in certain states, and you'll need to register again.

If you're not sure if you're registered, it's probably a good idea just to go ahead and register again. It doesn't cost anything and only takes a few minutes. It's better than possibly waiting in line for an hour or longer on Election Day only to find out that you aren't registered.

Even if you filled out a voter registration form somewhere, don't assume it definitely went through. Most of the volunteers who collect signatures in a grocery store parking lot or other public places are reliable, but others might forget to turn them in. Forms sometimes get lost. Or the state office might reject your registration, for innocent reasons or for less-than-innocent ones. If you're not sure, you can contact your state election office anytime before the election to check on whether you still need to register.

Luckily, some lawmakers have made it easier for people to register. In 1993 Congress passed the National Voter Registration Act, better known as the "Motor Voter Act," which went into effect in 1995. Among other things, the law required states to offer a voter registration application to anyone applying for or renewing a driver's license (hence the nickname), and to anyone applying for or renewing certain forms of government assistance (including food stamps, welfare, or disability services). It also required all states to accept federal registration forms and made it easier to register by mail. The idea was to get more people involved in the political process by letting them register when they were using a government service anyway, make it easier for voters to reregister if their information changed (for example, when they might already be updating the address on their licenses), and to make it harder for states to discriminate against disadvantaged people when it came to voting. It also saved government money by combining the processes, while cutting down on paperwork, so win-win.

As mentioned above, some states allow same-day registration (at least fifteen as of early 2019, with more considering it). That's also made it easier for people to vote, and in some instances it's helped battle attempts to discriminate against certain voters. But it can also make Election Day a long day. When Illinois tried same-day registration for the first time in 2014, some voters had waits as long as nine hours, and some polling places needed to stay open well past midnight. There's no way to know how many people gave up and just went home or back to work or what impact their votes would have had on the state's close gubernatorial race that year. (In May 2017, Illinois became the tenth state with automatic voter registration, meaning people who use certain state services are registered unless they opt out.) Think of same-day registration more as a backup plan than a first option; you're always better off registering by the regular deadline.

SOME PROBLEMS

To understand how serious registration issues can get, let's look at one of the most extreme examples. The 2000 presidential election in Florida will forever be infamous because it was such a fiasco, and twenty years later, it's worth remembering all the reasons why. People focused on how the Electoral College meant the popular vote winner lost the presidency, even though (as we've discussed) it isn't going to change as long as states have the power to block any reform. It's also still controversial that, even with many irregularities that could have changed the outcome of a close race, the Supreme Court stopped officials who were in the process of recounting the state's votes from finishing that job.

Not only did a close race in Florida—the official count had George W. Bush and Al Gore separated by just 537 votes out of almost six million cast in the state—change who got to be president, but there were also many problems with how Florida handled those votes. One of the biggest issues was that the Florida secretary of state's office purged the voter rolls, meaning a lot of eligible, registered voters showed up to vote on Election Day, only to be told they weren't allowed to do so.

SUPPRESSING THE VOTE

Ideally, government officials and parties would always try to win by appealing to the largest number of voters. In reality, some officials have decided it's easier to try to stop voters who don't support them from voting in the first place, a sleazy practice called *voter suppression*. Seventeen states had new voting restrictions in place during the 2016 election, many specifically designed to keep certain voters from being able to participate.

In 2011 Wisconsin governor Scott Walker pushed for a law requiring a current photo ID to vote. Though a federal court temporarily blocked the measure in 2014—noting that African American voters in Wisconsin were 50 percent less likely than white voters to have photo IDs—an appeals court let it go forward for the 2016 election. Partly because of the strict ID laws (for example, many forms of student ID were no longer allowed, nor was an expired license even if it had the owner's picture), Wisconsin saw its lowest voter turnout since 2000. In Milwaukee, the state's biggest city and a heavily Democratic area, turnout dropped by more than forty thousand from 2012, and other cities saw comparable drops. Not coincidentally, Donald Trump became the first Republican to win Wisconsin since 1984, with only about twenty-three thousand more votes than Hillary Clinton.

Not all voter-suppression efforts succeed. After the Supreme Court made the controversial 2013 decision to eliminate some parts of the 1965 Voting Rights Act, the North Carolina legislature passed sweeping changes to suppress votes: creating strict ID requirements, eliminating same-day registration, and dramatically reducing early voting. These efforts were so transparent that a federal appeals court ruled against the bill—state officials even admitted in court that they were trying to limit voting in disproportionately black counties—and the Supreme Court backed that decision.

Fortunately, many voters care enough about their rights to protest voter suppression. Unfortunately, some states keep giving them reasons to demonstrate.

Unfortunately, voter suppression made a big comeback in the 2018 midterms, in North Carolina and elsewhere. Georgia secretary of state Brian Kemp kicked more than 1.5 million registered voters off his state's rolls, closed polling places in primarily African American neighborhoods, and even discarded hundreds of absentee ballots without the proper notifications. The effort was not only nakedly partisan but also self-serving—Kemp was making rules about his own race for governor, helping him win by less than 2 percent of the vote.

He wasn't alone. North Dakota passed a law requiring voters to have an ID with a street address, a move made specifically to disenfranchise American Indian voters living on reservations, which often don't use street addresses. Several states closed or relocated polling places in minority-populated districts, passed complicated voter ID laws, or had discrepancies in how ballots were counted. Sadly, this nonsense has become routine, and it needs to be freshly combated every election cycle.

Another problem was that Florida had a law that prevented convicted felons from voting (a law that was not overturned until a 2018 referendum). It wasn't the only state where that was true—other states, including Iowa and Virginia, ban anyone convicted of a felony from ever voting again, unless the governor pardons them for their crime or the state specifically restores that person's voting rights. In most states, felons lose voting rights while they're in prison, but they can apply again after serving their sentence (how long after depends on the state), while Maine and Vermont never take away felons' voting rights. Florida felons could, of course, still try to register, but the law said their registrations wouldn't be valid.

Here's where things went bad. Florida's secretary of state, Katherine Harris, hired a private company to go through Florida's list of registered voters and find anyone convicted of a felony. The firm went pretty far beyond that, listing more than *170,000* registered Florida voters who it felt should lose their votes. Some were actually felons. Some were convicted of misdemeanors or charged with felonies but not convicted—but that wasn't supposed to matter as far as voting rights. Some were just people who had the same name as a convicted felon, or a similar name, and unfairly lost their ability to vote. One county election supervisor found her own name listed, even though she'd never been charged with a felony.

To make matters worse, each county in Florida could use the list differently. Some sent notices to the voters named, giving them a chance to appeal their removal. In other counties, voters never knew there was a problem until Election Day, when it was too late to do anything about it. It also wasn't a secret that Harris, who ordered the purge, was cochair of the Bush campaign in Florida, which was at best a conflict of interest. A few counties just refused to use the list at all, blaming its partisan origins . . . and, in the process, actually let a handful of convicted felons vote.

While the impact of Florida's problems on the presidential election was obviously a huge news story for a long time—for more than a month, the country didn't know who the president-elect was—having that many eligible voters unable to vote also affected every other election in Florida that year, from Congress to state offices to local offices, for which a few missing voters could make a huge difference.

Because the election was so close, state law required counties to recount their ballots, and the weeks-long process showed off some of the other issues with Florida's elections. Different counties used different voting systems on Election Day. Part of recounting votes meant looking at individual ballots and trying to fairly tally votes, but little decisions became big controversies when even a few votes in a county might elect a different president. One such example involved Palm Beach County's "butterfly ballot," which listed candidates on both the left and right of a central spine, with arrows pointing to which hole voters were supposed to punch. The recount showed more than two thousand voters who meant to vote for Gore, who was listed second on the left side, instead accidentally voted for Reform Party candidate Pat Buchanan, who was listed first on the right side and aligned to the second punch (and those voters didn't know about their mistake until it came up during the recount). Another recount controversy involved punch-card ballots, as the voter's choice wasn't counted if the ballot wasn't punched all the way through, and officials tried to manually determine what voters had meant to do.

The Bush-Gore election made Florida an obvious punching bag, but other states had some of the same problems. Just because they didn't swing the presidential election didn't mean they couldn't also use reform.

SOME FIXES

In 2002 Congress reacted to some of the problems with the Florida disaster by passing the Help America Vote Act (HAVA), which set out to fix several voting flaws across the country. There's a lot in the law, but a few fixes are worth mentioning. For one thing, it got rid of punch-card voting and eliminated voting by pulling a lever (an old-fashioned system many states had already stopped using). To address the county-by-county inconsistencies, it required states to keep all voter registrations in one statewide list and to make that list computerized, for easy searching and updating. It also mandated that every polling place have a way for disabled voters to participate. To avoid problems like the one with the butterfly ballot, HAVA required polling places to give voters a chance to review their vote before it was submitted and counted (and, if they or the machine made a mistake, a chance to change it).

HAVA also required every polling place to keep a paper trail, with records of all votes that can be used in case any election is close enough to require a recount. Recounts happen more often than you might think, including in the 2004 governor election in Washington State and the 2008 Senate race in Minnesota. Since lots of states switched to electronic voting machines, the paper trail became even more important, serving as the only backup in case a machine tabulated votes incorrectly or lost some of the data.

The law also required that states use provisional ballots. That means if the election staff at your polling place thinks you aren't registered or that your registration isn't valid, but you know that you signed up, you can still cast a vote that counts (once officials confirm that you're right). A few cases in which you might need a provisional ballot: if your state requires you to show an ID but you don't have it on you; if your name or address on your registration doesn't exactly match your official ID; or if your name isn't on the voter list for that polling place.

Provisional ballots often aren't counted on Election Day, so you're better off confirming your registration as mentioned earlier in this chapter. Plus, they can still be rejected by election officials, and you won't know for sure whether your vote counted, which is one of the most common criticisms of provisional ballots. That said, it's a better alternative than waiting in line, finding out your registration isn't listed, and getting turned away with a 0 percent chance of your vote counting.

Like any law, HAVA hasn't always been enforced perfectly, but it at least tried to solve some problems and made some progress. The law also created an independent agency—the Election Assistance Commission—that you can contact with complaints if you notice an issue. Unfortunately, states still sometimes try to get around the law, but at least it's now illegal instead of just unethical. In 2012 Florida had another controversial purge of its voter rolls, this time claiming to focus on noncitizens, and again removed lots of valid voters. But the new regulations meant a much smaller number of voters were invalidated, and a federal court later ruled that the purge itself was illegal.

Section II
Being an Informed Voter

Once you've registered, congratulations, you're able to vote in the next election. You just need to decide which candidates or parties will get your support.

Before you do that, you should educate yourself about the candidates, where they stand on the issues, what they've accomplished in their careers already, and what specific plans they have for after they take office.

Here's the thing. You don't *have* to be an informed voter; as you probably picked up from this book's introduction, the United States has no shortage of voters who truly don't know what they're talking about. There will always be a lot of them, and each one of them can cancel out the vote of someone who actually pays attention and makes informed decisions.

It's easy to be cynical about this reality, but that doesn't accomplish anything. There's only one solution. If more Americans become informed voters, especially young voters, they'll be able to outnumber the uninformed ones. It might take a while, but those numbers can add up. The 2008 election saw a big increase in the number of young people voting, so look at it this way: If citizens who turned eighteen and voted for the first time in 2008 make it to the average American life expectancy, they'll still be voting in the 2068 election. That's exactly the same time difference as between electing James Madison and Ulysses S. Grant, or between choosing Theodore Roosevelt and Lyndon Johnson. A generation that pays attention to politics and knows what it's talking about can make a difference for a long time.

MORE AND MORE INFO

Back when the United States was a new country, it could be hard to get information during a campaign. For a local election, it was easy enough to go to town meetings and hear what everyone had to say, and local newspapers were able to cover news while it was breaking. National news, on the other hand, could take a while, since long-distance information had to physically travel a long distance, either by boat, by riders on horseback, or by word-of-mouth conversation. In one famous example during the War of 1812, Andrew Jackson and his troops defeated some seventy-five hundred British soldiers in the Battle of New Orleans, a battle that was totally unnecessary—the agreement to end the war had been signed two weeks earlier, but word of the deal hadn't gotten to New Orleans in time for the British to call off the attack. As the country got bigger, news could travel even slower; getting information from the West Coast to the East Coast in the early nineteenth century could take weeks or even months and could require serious wilderness survival skills.

The good news is that technology has improved a lot since then, making it easier to get information a lot faster. Trains and then cars and then airplanes made the post office a lot faster. Radio and then TV made it possible to get news each night about what had happened that day, without needing to wait for the newspaper the next morning. In June of 1980, the literally named Cable News Network (or CNN) became the first twenty-four-hour news channel.

How fast things have changed since then is something that's easy to take for granted. As recently as 1979—not that long ago—even hard-core politics junkies could have no idea about a big story until a news broadcast at six or nine at night, unless they had an inside source or witnessed a news event personally. And serious analysis of political news usually had to wait until a newspaper arrived the next morning. Within just thirty years, it became normal for a news junkie to have access to several twenty-four-hour news channels, plus local and international news broadcasts on cable, plus websites for every major newspaper and magazine that update throughout the day, plus thousands of political blogs, plus satellite radio with all-news stations, plus social media such as Facebook, Twitter, Reddit, Snapchat, Instagram, and Tumblr. If you want to find information about any issue or candidate, it's out there and relatively easy to locate.

The bad news is that the same changes that make it easier to get news have also helped lies, conspiracy theories, and even innocently passed-along wrong information spread quickly and easily. Almost as soon as e-mail became a widespread thing, so did bogus chain e-mails full of urban legends. (See sidebar on page 150 for some places to debunk them.) Today, that's more likely to take the form of a quote or meme on social media that people "like" and pass along without knowing or caring whether it's real, or whether the argument even makes sense. That's especially common when it comes to politics. When discussing the subject, people have a tendency to present what they believe as a fact, even when you can easily prove it's not true.

One 2013 poll by the Public Policy Polling firm asked Americans about conspiracy theories and found the following terrifying information: 37 percent of respondents believed global warming to be a hoax, 28 percent believed former Iraqi dictator Saddam Hussein was involved in the September 11, 2001, attacks against the United States, and 4 percent thought shape-shifting lizard people have a hand in running the government. Even if those numbers were high, the fact that they weren't 0 percent in all cases is a problem. (For the record: sixteen of the seventeen hottest years in recorded history have happened since 2000; Saddam Hussein was an enemy of the al-Qaeda terrorist network that carried out the attacks, and not involved; and lizard people, really?) Those aren't cases of having a different opinion about a subject; those are cases of being objectively wrong. There's a difference between thinking that pizza from one restaurant is better than pizza from a different place (a matter of opinion, where either side can be right) and thinking one of those pizzas is actually a magical food you can use to travel back in time (a matter of fact, where one side is wrong . . . and kind of crazy).

Speaking of crazy, it's not as if things have gotten better since that poll. In 2015 the same firm conducted a poll in which 41 percent of self-identified Donald Trump supporters said they were good with the idea of bombing Agrabah—a country that exists only in Disney's *Aladdin*. After Russian agents hacked the Democratic National Committee's e-mails in 2016, and those e-mails were published online by Wikileaks, conspiracy nuts concocted an entire theory that the Hillary Clinton campaign's frequent pizza orders (a pretty normal thing for any campaign pulling a lot of long hours) were instead code for operating a sex-trafficking ring.

GETTING PAST FAKE NEWS

There's a lot of information flying about during a campaign. There's also a lot of misinformation, and it takes many forms.

Luckily, a few nonpartisan organizations do a good job of going through all that information for you and letting you know what's real, what's kind of true, and what's complete BS.

POLITIFACT (politifact.com): As the name suggests, this site run by the staff of the *Tampa Bay Times* focuses specifically on politics. Launched in 2007, PolitiFact looks at the validity of claims made by candidates, officials, media figures, and even bloggers, and ranks those claims on a "Truth-o-Meter" with a six-point scale—*true, mostly true, half true, mostly false, false,* and the ever-popular *pants on fire*. Every day, the site's staff finds claims it considers newsworthy enough to check out, and its work has earned PolitiFact a Pulitzer Prize.

FACTCHECK.ORG (factcheck.org): This site, run by the University of Pennsylvania's Annenberg Public Policy Center, also focuses on politics and policy. During presidential primaries and elections, it has pages devoted to all major candidates. FactCheck checks internet rumors (on its "Viral Spiral" page) and science-related claims, offers a news quiz, and has a mailbag where you can make suggestions about suspicious claims the site might want to check out.

SNOPES (snopes.com): Snopes isn't specifically for political news; it's an all-purpose site for debunking urban legends, rumors, scams, doctored photos, pseudohistory, and other forms of fakery. The site started in 1995—making it a few years older than Google—when the number of people using the internet for the first time was growing quickly, and that was making it easy for people to pass along (intentionally or unknowingly) chain e-mails full of lies. Snopes still does a nice job of shooting down conspiracy theories and dishonest memes, including political ones.

***WASHINGTON POST* FACT CHECKER** (washingtonpost.com/news/fact-checker): Starting in 2007, the *Post* has regularly published this nonpartisan column. It uses the newspaper's reporting resources to research and judge the accuracy of politicians' statements, with a scale based on how many "Pinocchios" the speaker earned. About half of its reports begin by investigating a question from a *Post* reader.

OPENSECRETS (opensecrets.org): If you want to follow the money, this is a great resource. The nonprofit Center for Responsive Politics (CRP) runs this site, which looks specifically at the role of money in politics. CRP was founded in the early 1980s by a pair of retired senators, Democrat Frank Church and Republican Hugh Scott, who were concerned about how big donors were influencing policy—which, as we'll cover later, has only become a bigger problem—and launched its OpenSecrets site in 1996. It lists every candidate's contributors, plus contributors to party committees, advocacy groups, and political action committees involved in elections for any federal office. The site also lets you search contributions by zip code, so you can find out if anyone you know contributes to candidates and, if so, who got their money.

Based on nothing. This rubbish wasn't harmless either; in December 2016, an armed man fired shots in a DC pizza place falsely accused of being part of the criminal activity that didn't exist.

To take a nonpolitical example, think about how many times celebrities are reported dead on Twitter, even though they are very much alive. Actor Morgan Freeman was a popular victim, wrongly declared dead on social media several times, even though he was both alive and still making movies. Or how many times people claimed the specific day on which they were posting was the one to which Marty McFly traveled in *Back to the Future II*—an altered-photo meme that went around social media a lot, in waves that started a few years before the actual day. In those cases, nobody was trying to spread the misinformation to benefit themselves; they just heard something interesting and shared it. Which would have been great . . . if what they had heard was true. Nobody gets hurt if people think *Back to the Future II* took place in 2013 instead of 2015. On the other hand, wrong information about government can have consequences, from tricking the public into supporting an unnecessary war to people voting out members of Congress based on positions they've never actually held.

An easy way to do your part is not to pass along bad information and to check out any info that seems fishy before you spread it. Social media platforms work on algorithms, so sharing a dishonest or inaccurate post—even if you're debunking it or adding a comment about how it's wrong—still helps that false information gain traffic. Plus, posting stuff that's easily disprovable makes it easier for people to dismiss the accurate and important things you share on the same subject. Also, if you post or forward something that turns out not to be true, do everybody a favor and delete the original post. Whatever social media platform you use, you've probably seen things in your news feed that someone in the comments has proven wrong, and the person who posted it apologized for sharing—but for some reason, that person kept the post there. People scrolling through their feed might not read the comments and might believe something untrue just because a trusted friend shared it. News publications make these kinds of corrections online all the time. They'll fix published stories if they find errors and usually add a note explaining that the story was updated and why. You can do the same thing and help keep wrong information away from your friends and family. (And if your friends and family share false information, don't be afraid to call it out, especially if you can back it up. You're not doing them a favor by ignoring bad information.)

During the 2016 election cycle, the term *fake news* became a popular meme—and an often-misused one. Both as a candidate and while in the White House, Donald Trump routinely used this term, as the fact-checking site PolitiFact put it, "to describe news coverage that is unsympathetic to his administration and his performance, even when the news reports are accurate." His warping of the term into an attack on anyone who doesn't agree with him led others to repeat the same tactic, but it's important to remember that there's a big difference between news you don't like, or that doesn't tell you what you want to hear, and news that's actually fake.

One of the ways the Russian government worked to influence the 2016 election was to create phony social media accounts or bots to spread actual fake news. One Twitter profile revealed as a fake had more than twenty-two thousand followers, while one Russian "troll farm" purchased more than three thousand Facebook ads that were seen by millions of people. Some fake news sites tried to look and feel like real news sites (Bloomberg, ABC News, and NBC News were among the sources trolls tried to mimic), while others just claimed to have information that "the mainstream media doesn't want you to know," or similar clickbait nonsense. Of course, not all fake news is that coordinated. Sometimes it's just blog posts or tweets passed along by someone who doesn't know or doesn't care that the information is a lie.

The point here isn't that you should vote for or against any particular candidate or party. But you should at least know *why* you're voting for and against them and do that for actual, honest reasons. If you vote against someone because you disagree with their actual stances on issues or something they actually did or said, you're just doing your job as a voter. If you vote against the same person because you believed some conspiracy theory about them that you read on a discredited social media post, then you're part of the problem. As former senator Daniel Patrick Moynihan put it, "Everyone is entitled to his own opinion but not to his own facts."

WHERE TO GET YOUR INFORMATION

So now that we've talked about what *not* to do, what should you do to educate yourself about politics?

Technology has made heaps of sources easily accessible, many of them free (or at least inexpensive). When it comes to news sites, or places claiming to be news sites, consider the source. And your best bet is to get your news from a mix of sources.

An often-cited 2007 Pew Study found that people who got their news from Comedy Central's *Daily Show with Jon Stewart* and *The Colbert Report* did much better on an objective news quiz than people who got their news from other TV shows (especially the openly partisan Fox News, local TV news, and fluffy network morning shows). Stewart retired and Colbert switched to a late-night talk show in 2015. However, readers of major newspaper websites also performed at the top of that study, and viewers of the Public Broadcasting System (PBS) news weren't far behind. Good information has less to do with the format of the delivery method than with the people collecting and presenting it.

Getting a newspaper delivered every morning isn't nearly as common as it was even ten years ago, but newspaper, wire service, and magazine reporters are still some of the best sources for fair reporting and political analysis, and you can read their work on the publications' websites and social media accounts (and the writers' own). Many of the blogs or columns you might read still heavily rely on newspaper journalists' work, writing analysis or commentary on stories that traditional journalists investigated and reported.

The country's major newspapers, including the *New York Times*, *Washington Post*, *Los Angeles Times*, and *Chicago Tribune* cover what's going on in Washington, DC, as well as in the city where they're based. People who don't understand how news works sometimes act like a newspaper's op-ed section makes its reporting biased, but that's nonsense. That the *New York Times* publishes more liberal and moderate columnists than conservative ones doesn't change the excellent job done by most of its news reporters, and the *Wall Street Journal*'s serious reporters aren't any less accurate because the op-ed page is famously far to the right. Op-ed pages can be useful resources to find out what columnists with certain perspectives think about the news; just keep in mind where the columnists are coming from.

Wire services such as the Associated Press, Reuters, and United Press International have reporters all over the globe whose job is to accurately report what's happening and make those stories available worldwide. Wire service stories regularly wind up in news publications. If you read a reported article from overseas or from Washington in a small local newspaper, you'll usually see a wire service listed under the writer's name. Those stories are also easily available online, both through the wire service's online presence and through aggregators such as Google News and Yahoo! News.

Thanks to the web and social media, you can read how international newspapers cover American elections and politics (though they focus mostly on the presidential and congressional elections). Papers such as the *Guardian* (from the United Kingdom), the *Sydney Morning Herald* (from Australia), and the *Toronto Star* (from Canada) are just some of the dozens of English-language papers that have reporters in the United States, and that you can read online to get another perspective on US politics. That's something older generations didn't have. And if you read other languages, that gives you many more options.

There are also tons of magazines that either specifically cover politics or cover it as one of many subjects. There isn't room here to list every magazine worth checking out, but some good options include *Rolling Stone*, the *New Yorker*, the *Atlantic*, the *Economist*, *Esquire*, *Mother Jones*, the *New York Times Magazine*, *Foreign Policy*,

Politico, the *New Republic*, *Slate*, the *Week*, *Time*, and many others. There are plenty of city-specific or state-specific magazines as well. Like columnists, some political magazines come from a particular political viewpoint, so that's worth keeping in mind. Blogs and social media sites can be really great resources and fun to read, if you're careful about which ones you choose and read them with a skeptical eye. The good ones will include links to the sites and articles they use as sources, and following those links is a smart way to pick up extra context.

TV news is probably the most obvious source to consider, whether it's CNN, the broadcast networks (NBC, CBS, ABC), PBS, or the partisan networks such as Fox News. Not only do those networks have daily (or, in some cases, all-day) newscasts, but national candidates appear on Sunday morning talk shows, late-night network talk shows, and even comedy programs such as the *Daily Show*, *Last Week Tonight*, *Full Frontal with Samantha Bee*, and *Real Time with Bill Maher*. Or you can get an international take on American politics from the BBC, Al-Jazeera, France 24, and other overseas news channels. All those networks and shows post clips online, on YouTube, and via social media.

For national and some state races, you can watch debates between the candidates on live TV. We'll talk more about debates in the next chapter, but they're the one situation in which candidates have to react to one another face-to-face.

The cable network C-SPAN (Cable-Satellite Public Affairs Network) was created to broadcast the day-to-day work of Congress, which it still does. It also broadcasts most major speeches and appearances by national candidates or state candidates in races that receive national attention (for example, Senate and governor races that are competitive or feature candidates the channel considers notable). That coverage is accessible for free at C-SPAN.org and will give you more information than the few snippets of a speech you might see on other TV news networks.

Of course, in an election year, your state and local races probably won't receive much coverage in major outlets outside your home state. No matter where you live, your local newspaper or news site will be your best choice for keeping up with races closer to home. The same goes for your local TV and radio stations.

Another good way to find out what candidates support is to look at what they say about themselves. As we covered earlier, parties have platforms that explain what their leadership hopes to achieve or prevent. Every candidate at the national and state level, and all but the most technophobic of them at the local level, likely have a website where they (or, usually, their staff) post their positions on issues, information about their schedules, and their biographies. Smart campaign managers have embraced social media, letting campaigns and candidates send information directly to you through Twitter, Instagram, Facebook, and other apps and services.

Naturally, that's a way to find out what candidates want to communicate, but you can also use news resources to see if they've lived up to what they're saying. If a candidate says he has always supported a particular program, that isn't a case where you just have to take his word. You can look it up. It's fine if candidates change their opinions about something when the situation changes or they can explain why they switched. But if they claim one thing and their voting record says another, or if they supported policies that turned out to be a disaster, that's a perfectly valid thing to think about when deciding whether they earned your vote. If there's one takeaway here, it's that nonpartisan journalism is your best resource for information about politics.

If you combine hard news from quality papers, analysis from outlets with different political views, information from the candidates and parties, and fact-checking sites, you'll wind up knowing much more about what's going on than the average voter does.

Section III
Showing Up

All the preparation we've covered in this chapter is great, but it only counts if the voters who register turn up to vote in the election. Not just for the November presidential election, but during primaries. And during midterm elections and off-year elections. And not just for the big races for president and governor, but for state representative and mayor and county commissioner. The smaller the race, the larger the percentage of the vote you can influence directly.

Parties, special interest groups, and local candidates all understand this and hold get-out-the-vote drives on Election Day. They call and send e-mail reminders to people they consider supporters, reminding them to vote. In some cases, they even arrange volunteer car pools or buses to take voters physically to the polls.

There are tons of things that can drive down turnout, from rain or snow on Election Day, to polls that show certain important races aren't competitive, to general voter apathy. The 2014 midterm election saw only 36.4 percent of Americans vote, the lowest percentage in more than seventy years—back when one of

AROUND THE WORLD

Voter turnout in the United States is famously low when compared to other Western democratic countries (some of which, to be fair, make voting mandatory). In May 2017, the Pew Research Center charted turnout for the last national election in those countries.

Even though the study counted the 2016 presidential election for the United States (when turnout among the voting-age population was much better than in the 2014 midterm), this country still trailed many others when it came to the percentage of people who voted. But the United States did a lot better when it came to the percentage of the people who registered to vote actually voting.

Here's the top ten for those categories:

HIGHEST PERCENTAGE OF VOTER TURNOUT AMONG THE VOTING-AGE POPULATION		HIGHEST PERCENTAGE OF VOTER TURNOUT AMONG REGISTERED VOTERS	
Belgium	87.2	Luxembourg	91.1
Sweden	82.6	Australia	91.0
Denmark	80.3	Belgium	89.4
Australia	79.0	United States	86.8
Norway	78.0	Denmark	85.9
South Korea	77.9	Sweden	85.8
Netherlands	77.3	Turkey	85.4
Iceland	76.8	Netherlands	81.9
Israel	76.1	Iceland	79.2
New Zealand	73.2	Norway	78.3

the excuses for not voting was "off fighting World War II." That statistic received a lot of attention at the time and for good reason. Fewer than four in ten Americans were deciding who would get to make laws that the nonvoting majority would have to live with.

One fact that received less attention? Even that embarrassingly low number actually meant 64.9 percent of registered voters took part in the election. That means the issue had more to do with eligible voters not even registering to use that vote than it did with registered voters not showing up, and it's reasonable to think that increasing registration is the best way to increase turnout. (See chart on page 160.)

There are definite trends in who votes, and candidates know that. It's been a common complaint about politics for a while that the country spends a lot more money on retirees than it does on young voters. For example, programs such as Social Security and Medicare, which are primarily for Americans over sixty-five, are funded by the government. In 2003 an expensive prescription-drug component was added to Medicare at taxpayer expense. Meanwhile, healthcare and public college are free for everyone in much of the world, but here the government's role in terms of young people is to give them access to health insurance and student loans, both of which can be really expensive.

One factor in that split is that older Americans turn out to vote at much greater rates than younger voters. That makes it harder for candidates to propose policies that would anger large numbers of older voters, and it's more difficult to take action on a beneficial but expensive program that helps younger Americans if there's a feeling that they won't show up to support it.

From 1988 to 2012, according to the Pew Research Center,

the voter turnout among Americans aged eighteen to twenty-four was highest in 1992 (48.6 percent) and 2008 (48.5 percent). Those were the first presidential elections for Bill Clinton and Barack Obama, respectively, two relatively young candidates (both in their forties at the time) who fared well with young voters. Turnout by young people was less impressive in 1988 (39.9 percent), 1996 (35.6 percent), 2000 (36.1 percent), and even 2012 (41.2 percent). And that's in presidential elections, when turnout is at its highest.

For the sake of comparison, the percentage of Americans sixty-five and older who showed up isn't just higher; it's a lot higher. In 1992, 75.1 percent of them voted, and the *lowest* turnout in that age bracket from 1988 to 2012 was 69.1 percent—more than 20 percent better than the best youth turnout in that span. So can you really blame politicians for allocating tax dollars to the issues elderly voters care about?

Plus, as we covered earlier, state and local elections can affect you even more directly than federal ones. If they happen in a non-presidential year, they suffer from even lower turnout. While the 2014 turnout mentioned above was really low overall, it was even lower in states where there wasn't a high-profile race for governor or senator. Maine was picking a governor in a controversial election that year, so more than 58 percent of the state voted. In Indiana, where the House of Representatives was the highest office up for a vote, turnout was below 29 percent, and New York wasn't much better. Midterm electorates tend to be older and whiter than electorates in presidential years, and for better or worse, that makes a difference in who gets elected.

The good news for you as a young voter is there are potentially a lot of you. Adults born after 1980, according to the most recent census, already make up one quarter of the voting-age population. Because the baby boomers are now past retirement age, "millennials" (and those too young to call themselves by that term) are becoming an even bigger percentage; the Census Bureau predicts that the post-1980 generation will hit 36.5 percent of eligible voters by 2020.

The numbers show a more ethnically diverse electorate coming soon too. The 2012 election was the first time in American history in which a higher percentage of black Americans than white Americans voted (66.2 to 64.1 percent), though Latino turnout was far lower (about 48 percent). The country's demographic changes mean that, per the Census Bureau, people of color are expected to be 37.2 percent of eligible voters by 2020, and *54.8* percent by 2060. As with young voters, a common complaint about politics is that voters of color are sometimes ignored or taken for granted by politicians. But just as with young voters, the numbers are there to change that, if turnout follows.

ELECTING BEFORE ELECTION DAY

Election Day is always going to be the most important day on the campaign calendar, but once again, depending on where you live, you might be able to vote before that day.

In attempts to increase turnout, many states have gradually started to think of Election Day more as a deadline than as a one-time-only event.

Back when the concept of voting on the first Tuesday after the first Monday in November was introduced, the small number of eligible voters often had to travel great distances to vote, so it

DIRTY TRICKS

As mentioned earlier, lots of good organizations run registration drives to get more people to vote, with the idea that the country's more democratic if more people take part. On the other hand, there will always be some campaigns that know they have a disadvantage if voter turnout is high. In a few cases, those campaigns (or other forces that support those campaigns, with or without permission) try to solve that problem by decreasing turnout.

Sometimes, suppression can mean officials kicking eligible voters off the rolls (as in Florida in 2000), or states passing laws that require only certain forms of ID to vote (as in Wisconsin). Other times, it's as simple as lying and trying to trick people into staying home.

In 2012 Paul Schurick, the campaign manager for Maryland governor Bob Ehrlich, Jr. was found guilty of an illegal attempt to suppress the African American vote during the governor's 2010 reelection bid. More than one hundred thousand voters in two primarily black counties received automated "robocalls" on Election Day telling them they could "relax" because Democratic challenger Martin O'Malley had already won. Except he hadn't yet, and this was a trick to convince his supporters that they didn't need to show up. In that case, at least, the cheating failed. Ehrlich lost the election, and though Schurick avoided jail time, he was sentenced to four

made sense to have a target day when everyone would convene in one place. Now the country has many more voters, many of them working jobs where it's hard to slip out to vote during a weekday, and states have tried to make it easier for them to participate.

years' probation and five hundred hours of community service.

In 2008 voters in one Virginia district with a close congressional race received flyers saying that due to "larger than expected voter turnout," Democrats and independents should vote on November 5, and Republicans on November 4. A similar ruse in 2004 involved fliers being passed out in African American neighborhoods telling voters to make sure to vote on November 3 . . . the only problem being that Election Day was actually November 2 that year. Just to be clear, if anyone tells you Election Day is pushed back for any reason, they're full of it, you shouldn't believe them, and it's a good idea to let other people know it's not true.

In other examples, voters received phone calls on Election Day telling them their polling place location had changed when it hadn't, messages telling them certain elections were over while voting was still happening, threats that they would be arrested if they tried to vote while having unpaid parking tickets, or even intimidation outside a polling place. There's no way to quantify how many voters over the years have believed scams like these, or how many elections ended with a different result because of them. In many cases, we'll probably never even know who was behind them. So keep an eye out for these kinds of dirty tricks.

....

Oregon introduced a creative solution, with all voting done by mail. The state has had some form of by-mail voting since 1981, when state law first gave counties the option to use it. In 1998 Oregonians got to vote (via a ballot initiative on Election

Day) for whether the state should just use mail ballots for everything, and more than two-thirds of them said yes. Three weeks before Election Day, all Oregon voters receive a ballot in the mail, along with a pamphlet about all the candidates and initiatives on that ballot. All ballots must be returned by 8 p.m. on Election Day, by mail or in person, and only after that deadline are they counted. The system was popular enough that other states—first Washington in 2011, then Colorado in 2013, and California starting in 2018—also switched all their elections to vote-by-mail systems. A few other states use mail voting only for certain elections.

Mail voting is definitely more convenient. You can fill out your ballot whenever you want over the course of a few weeks and then just mail it back. It's cheaper too, since states don't have to set up and staff polling places. In Oregon and Washington, where it's three hours earlier than on the East Coast, it also cuts down on early results back East influencing whether voters show up (which used to be an issue when the presidential election was a blowout). Still, it isn't without its flaws. Washington's system requires ballots to be postmarked by Election Day—not turned in by then—so the state's results aren't official until a few days after the election.

More importantly, by-mail voting opens the possibility of your ballot not being private. At an in-person polling place, your ballot is guaranteed to be secret, which is an important part of American democracy. You can vote in whatever way you choose, and nobody else will know unless you tell them. People outside the polling place can ask you to support their candidate or ballot initiative (as long as they stand at least a certain distance away), but nobody inside the polling place can ask you to vote a certain way or look over your shoulder while you vote. When people are voting from anywhere at any time, on the other hand, it's easier for parents or friends to pressure them into voting a certain way or even fill out the ballot for someone else without their permission, and there's no way for the state to guarantee that the voter made his or her own choices.

Instead of going that route, many other states simply offer early voting, meaning polling places open a certain number of days before Election Day. In those states, you vote the same way you would otherwise. You go to your polling place, take a ballot, and fill it out in a private area. As of the 2016 election cycle, thirty-three states (plus Washington, DC) allowed early voting, and by 2008, 30.8 percent of ballots were cast early. Here, too, states have their own rules. Twenty-two of those states (plus DC again) have at least some early voting on the weekend. There's also variety as far as just how early that voting starts, from a month and a half before Election Day to just a few days beforehand. It can make the actual day of the election feel like less of an event, but it gives voters a much better chance of being able to participate.

We briefly mentioned absentee voting earlier, and that's another way to vote before Election Day. Every state has some form of an absentee ballot, which voters can request if they're not going to be around to vote in person. The majority of states (twenty-seven as of 2019, plus Washington, DC) offer "no-excuse" absentee voting. It's exactly what it sounds like—you just request a ballot in advance and don't have to give a reason why you can't show up at the polls. Twenty-one others will let you vote absentee but require an excuse before they'll let you do it (being away at college is a valid excuse; wanting to sleep in on Election Day, not so much).

A handful of states—including Arizona, California, Hawaii, Minnesota, Montana, New Jersey, and Utah (plus DC)—offer something called *permanent absentee voting*, meaning you can sign up to always have your ballot automatically sent to you by mail. (Several other states will allow you to do this only if you have a permanent disability. Alaska lets you do it if you live somewhere so remote and inaccessible that not being able to get to a polling place is a genuine problem.)

The goal of all these early approaches is to make it easier for as many Americans as possible to vote. The more Americans take part, the more representative the federal, state, and municipal governments will be. One side advantage is that early voting also makes counting votes on Election Day easier, so the public knows results sooner. Not the point, but a nice bonus.

Otherwise, if you live in a state where those aren't options, or if you simply want to vote on Election Day, you just follow the standard procedure. Find the location of your polling place, which should be mailed to you with your voter registration or which you can look up online. On the day of the primary or general election, you go to your polling place (usually a building like your local school or post office), a volunteer will check your name off a list, and you'll go into a private booth to make your choices. Double-check your ballot, turn it in, and you're officially a voter.

You'll also probably get a sticker or bracelet telling everybody you voted, which could make the absentee voters a little jealous.

Okay, now you should have the basic information you need to vote confidently, but there's more to elections than simply voting. In the next chapter, we'll talk about some aspects of campaigns and elections we haven't covered in depth yet. Once that's done, the final chapter will give you more options for how to get involved in elections, both now and in the future. ■

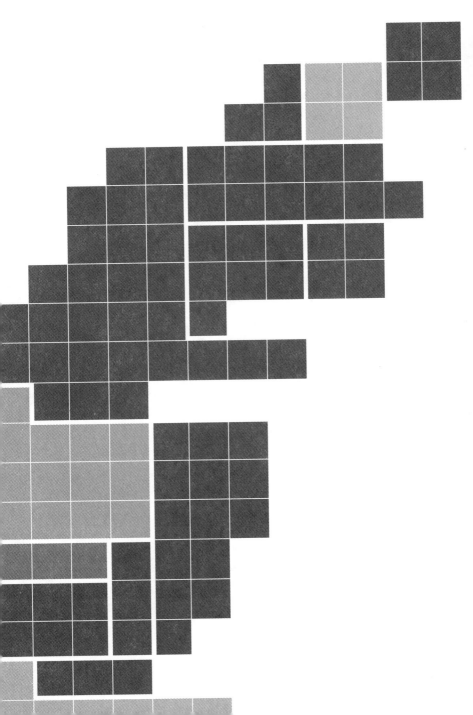

CHAPTER 5

WHAT'S GOING ON? POLLS, DEBATES, MONEY, AND BALLOT MEASURES

When it comes to the election process in the United States, one thing everyone can agree about is that the whole experience goes on a bit.

For one thing, it takes much more time to run for president here than it does for similar jobs in most of the world's democracies. The 2015 Canadian election campaign took seventy-eight days, longer than that country's two previous election cycles combined. In the United Kingdom, Prime Minister Theresa May called an election on April 19, 2017, and voters went to the polls on June 8. On February 1 the same year, New Zealand's prime minister announced an election with a September 23 date.

By American standards, that barely qualifies as a warm-up.

In the United States, the process has extended to the point that the first debate of the 2016 election was held on August 6, 2015—fifteen months before the November election (and a full six months before the Iowa caucuses kicked off the primary schedule). The first debate of the 2020 cycle was held even earlier, on June 26, 2019. Several candidates saw their presidential runs end months before any voters had a chance to decide their fate.

We've already talked a lot about the election process itself, but there are many aspects of elections that we've only touched on briefly that can play significant roles in how things play out. Over a long election cycle, topics such as public opinion and fundraising are ongoing processes, and they can change who winds up winning once the cycle finally wraps up. In this chapter, we'll talk about those and other parts of the election process in a bit more depth.

Section I
Polling

Polls have come up a few times in this book already. Basically, they're surveys that measure public opinion. That said, there are a variety of polls, with different methods and purposes.

Polls aren't specific to politics and government. Businesses use polls for market research, and polling firms also interview people about things like pop culture or purchasing habits. To keep things simple, however, this book is just going to discuss polls in terms of how they relate to politics. You'll hear a lot about them during any election, especially at the federal and state levels, so it's a good idea to understand how they work and what they measure.

Polls might look at a particular political race, asking potential voters which candidate they plan to support, how they rank the different candidates on specific issues, or who they think has the best chance of winning. That might be done specifically to predict a winner or to gauge voters' feelings along the way. In other cases, they might look at the performance of politicians currently in office, such as whether people approve of the job a president or governor is doing (that's where their approval rating comes from), how they view his or her performance on particular issues, and how they feel about ideas that person has proposed. Polls might also measure what Americans think about a range of political issues, such as gun laws or healthcare or the environment, without even mentioning any candidate or official. Or they might simply survey Americans' knowledge about the country, which is how we got the statistics in the introduction to this book.

When it comes to government and elections, the most useful polls are the ones that use a scientific method to try to obtain unbiased data about what the American people believe. That's the goal of the more well-known polling firms, and some of them have been in the game awhile. The Gallup Organization is considered the first modern polling firm and has conducted scientific public-opinion polls since the 1930s—it correctly predicted Franklin Roosevelt's landslide reelection victory in 1936 (admittedly, not the hardest prediction). Zogby International started surveying voters in the 1980s, and the Pew Research Center began in 1990. Those are just a few of the professional polling organizations trying to get unbiased data, and news organizations often conduct their own similar polls (sometimes partnering with other news organizations or with polling firms).

Interviewing every American about an issue is obviously an

impossible logistical nightmare, so pollsters instead try to interview a representative sample of the overall population they're trying to measure. Depending on the poll, that might mean trying to get a sense of all Americans or of a particular subset. When it comes to political issues, polls might measure everyone, or they might focus only on registered voters or *likely voters* (voters with a history of turning out on Election Day). Some might specifically interview Democrats or Republicans or independents. If the poll is about a race for governor or senator, it's only going to look at the state where that race is happening.

How each of the dozens of active polling firms creates its sample, including how it finds the people to contact, is generally a trade secret. After all, how close their predictions come to the actual outcome of an election is a big part of how they stand out from their competitors. But in all cases, they're trying to use probability to create the most representative sample possible. The industry standard for national polls is that about fifteen hundred respondents or more should be interviewed (though that number's not set in stone, and samples are usually much larger than that).

Polls are usually conducted by phone. A number of interviewers working for a pollster will call numbers from the list put together for the sample and ask the same series of questions to anyone who answers the call and agrees to take the survey. Once the poll questions are complete, the interviewer asks the respondents for demographic information, such as their age, race, gender, or party affiliation.

The data from all interviewees are then collected and analyzed, and the polling firm will sometimes use demographic data to weigh responses and make the sample as representative of the population as possible. For example, if the people who agree to take a certain poll are mostly male, but the overall population being surveyed is mostly female, some pollsters might count the responses from women more heavily in the final results. During any poll, a certain percentage of calls will go unanswered or will be answered by people who don't want to take the survey, and that affects how representative the sample can be.

In the process, pollsters calculate a margin of error, which uses probability to gauge the accuracy of the numbers found through the poll. The more representative a sample the pollster feels his or her survey actually reached, the smaller the margin of error will be, and vice versa. For example, if a poll shows a candidate has support from 65 percent of voters, and the margin of error is listed as 7 percent, that means the pollster conducting the survey believes the actual number is somewhere between 58 and 72 percent. If a poll shows a split of 51 to 49 percent, with a 2 percent margin of error, that means it actually shows that the race is a toss-up.

It became a popular (but misleading) talking point after the 2016 election that all polls showed Hillary Clinton was going to win. Even leaving her popular-vote victory aside, what the polls actually showed was that her odds of winning were fairly high, which is similar, but the difference is important. Most polls gave her a one-in-five chance of losing. That's a greater likelihood than rolling a one when you roll a six-sided die. It's more likely you'll get a different number, but that doesn't mean you won't roll a one.

Telephone polling is the most common technique, but pollsters also conduct in-person, face-to-face interviews with samples of voters. Sometimes, those involve one-on-one meetings for longer, in-depth interviews. In other cases, pollsters will put together focus groups, which bring several voters together in one room, and ask them questions.

All of that describes pollsters who are trying to put together unbiased data. In addition to those, there are professional polling firms that are allied (either intellectually or officially) with one political party or another. National parties conduct their own polls, as do presidential campaigns, the White House, and campaigns for any number of other offices. Those kinds of polls usually have an agenda beyond just straight opinion polling, whether it's testing support for a particular policy or introducing voters to an idea before a candidate starts talking about it.

WHY POLLS MATTER

Public-opinion polling informs government policy in numerous ways. Like any tool, it can have good or bad impacts, depending on how the polling data are used.

On the good side of the ledger, polling is the best way to understand how the American people in general feel about what's going on in the country (or at least the best way anybody's developed yet). It lets officials and candidates know whether their ideas are popular or unpopular, as well as the reasons why. It drives a lot of news coverage, because in a country where the will of the people is supposed to influence how government does its job, it's a way to explain what that will supports at that moment.

If the public seems skeptical about an idea, that might inspire a politician to do a better job explaining the details. If the public overwhelmingly supports a bill that's facing opposition in Congress, it might make some members of the House or Senate more willing to back its passage. Especially at the local level, where it's easier to get a representative sample of voters and a smaller number of voters changing sides can swing an election, polling can really influence what elected officials try to get done.

Generally, public opinion can help officials prioritize among the many issues on their plates. During an election, polls focused on who voters support can also be a huge help to campaigns, because they let candidates know where they stand and can help them plan accordingly. Politicians often claim that they don't read polls. Maybe they don't do it personally, but somebody on their staff definitely does, and it would be foolish if they didn't. Nobody needs to take polls as gospel or change anything based on them, but they're still useful data to consider. Plus, it must be said that, when it comes to predicting a winner, polls close to an election usually do a fairly good job.

On the other hand, polls can add to the horse-race nature of some political analysis, where who's winning or losing in the polls at a particular moment can become a bigger news story than what those candidates want to do. Also, while politicians responding to the public is sometimes a positive thing, it should also be important for leaders to do what's right instead of simply what's popular and to think about the long term. The public doesn't necessarily know or understand all of the options. As Henry Ford put it when describing the first car he built, if he'd asked people what they wanted, they would have asked for faster horses.

Polls can, unfortunately, influence voting behavior. In some cases, people don't show up to vote for a candidate they think is going to lose anyway, and in the process they help ensure that they're right about that. The reverse *boomerang effect* can also be true, meaning people are so sure their candidate is going to win

LANGUAGE MATTERS

Polls can also influence the words politicians use. Since the 1990s, it has become standard practice for politicians to poll the public about language and then use words that specifically appeal to their bases. In 1990 Representative Newt Gingrich hired pollsters to find out what words voters found positive or negative and encouraged other Republican candidates to constantly use these "words that work" in ads and speeches, either to make their own ideas more popular or make their opponents' less so. The practice got a boost after Gingrich led his party to victory in the 1994 midterm elections and became Speaker of the House.

It has since become common for supporters or opponents of certain laws or programs to label them in a way that will influence voters' perceptions. For example, the estate tax became less popular with the general public when opponents nicknamed it the "death tax" and repeated that wording over and over, even though the tax only applies to about the wealthiest 0.2 percent of inherited estates,

that they don't feel a need to vote . . . and enough people feeling that way can flip the outcome.

Another unfortunate tendency is that when polls ask voters their opinions on things that are matters of fact, the results are sometimes treated (by politicians and even some media outlets) as if people being wrong makes the facts less true. The previous chapter includes an example of a poll that found a significant number of Americans who believed provably wrong information about climate change or the September 11 attacks. That poll

and not the 100 percent of Americans who eventually die. In another famous example, a number of polls showed many more Americans supported the Affordable Care Act than supported "Obamacare"—even though the first is the actual name of the law, and the latter is a nickname for the exact same law.

After the terrorist attacks of September 11, 2001, Congress passed a wide-ranging law called the Uniting and Strengthening America by Providing Appropriate Tools Required to Intercept and Obstruct Terrorism Act—a tortured way to make the name fit the acronym USA PATRIOT Act, which would be hard for anyone to vote against with the 2002 election coming up. (You can imagine the attack ads: "Congressperson X says he loves America, so why does he oppose the PATRIOT Act?") The law received a lot of criticism, even at the time, for going too far in its surveillance of American citizens and the collection of their personal information, but only one senator out of one hundred (Democrat Russ Feingold of Wisconsin) voted against it.

....

demonstrated ignorance on the part of those respondents, but it also gave people a safety-in-numbers feeling for believing things that were complete BS, and some politicians have benefited by reinforcing wrong information as a way to win votes.

When evaluating poll data, it's also important to look at how the question was worded. For example, if a question just asks whether voters think a certain policy is working, saying no doesn't mean they oppose that policy in principle. They might support the idea but not the execution. Or they might think the policy goes too far, or not far enough, but both of those sides could be treated the same way in the data. To take a different example, a poll might ask voters to select what they consider a first choice among many options. They might like three other choices almost as much, or they might like just their first option. People who only read headlines about poll results can miss nuances like that, or the full data might not be widely reported.

Of course, who answers the polls also makes a huge difference in their outcome. Pollsters try to find as representative a sample as they can, but they can only do so much.

One problem that pollsters have really struggled with is the switch from landlines to mobile phones. As recently as 2003, more than 40 percent of American homes only used a landline for their phone service; by 2013, that number had fallen to below 10 percent. That's tough on pollsters for a few reasons. For one, federal law means automated dialing machines can't be used to call mobile phones, so anyone without a landline only counts in polls that involve interviewers manually dialing the numbers. For another thing, landlines always use a local area code, while people can keep the same mobile number no matter how often or where they move. A 310 area code on a landline means that number is in the Los Angeles area, but a 310 mobile phone could be located anywhere in the country, which can be a problem if someone's specifically trying to poll California voters.

Many pollsters believe that online surveys will eventually need to replace phone surveys as the main source of public-opinion information. Polling firms are working to develop ways of conducting online surveys that will be more representative, but as of this writing, that's still a work in progress.

The difficulty of reaching mobile phones has also made it harder to reach younger voters, because it's become normal for people to grow up without ever having a landline in their home. Because of that, polls often overweigh the responses of the young people who do respond, and the lower numbers are by definition less representative than the numbers for other age groups. Instead, some pollsters simply include fewer young voters in the data.

So if polls include more voices from older voters (and that is often what happens), the easiest solution is for more young people to answer their phones when a pollster calls and spend the few minutes it takes to answer the survey. Love them or hate them, as long as polls are the most popular tool for gauging citizens' sentiments, those who take part will always have a better chance of having their views count as part of public opinion.

TYPES OF POLLS

The standard, one-time phone poll we just discussed is still the most common form, but not the only type of poll used during an election campaign.

Tracking polls look at the same issues over a specific period of time, usually a few consecutive days, for the purpose of tracking how day-to-day events change public perception. They're particularly useful around something like a major policy speech or a debate, because they can show how the public reacted to the same question before, during, and after the event. Tracking polls might survey the same people over time or involve different people in similar samples.

Rapid-response surveys are conducted during or immediately after an event to measure the first impressions of its impact. For

DIRTY TRICKS, DISGUISED AS POLLS

One of the sleaziest of political dirty tricks is push polling, a propaganda technique that isn't actually polling at all. Instead, it's when people call citizens to introduce false information about one candidate, and the information is presented as a question (usually while the callers are pretending to be pollsters, hence the name).

Richard Nixon usually gets the credit and blame for the first use of push polling, during his 1946 race for a House seat from California. Voters received anonymous phone calls asking if they knew that Nixon's opponent, incumbent Democratic representative Jerry Voorhis, was a Communist. Then the caller hung up. Because this was decades before caller ID, it wasn't clear who was behind it, until a woman later admitted that the Nixon campaign had paid her to do it. Of course, Voorhis wasn't a Communist, but the calls put the idea in the heads of many voters. It's impossible to know how big a role that played in Nixon defeating Voorhis in an upset, but there were people who saw the underhanded tactic as helping launch a future president's career. Most campaigns consider it beneath them, so it doesn't always happen, but push polling has been used many times.

Now it's more common for push polls to identify themselves as

....

example, during televised presidential debates, networks often host focus groups that include undecided voters, supporters of each of the candidates, or both, and ask them all to turn dials to indicate when speakers say something the participants like or don't like. Another example is flash polls, which are phone polls conducted

coming from a real-sounding but fake polling firm and to phrase their smears against the candidate as questions.

Probably the most famous example of push polling was used against Senator John McCain during the 2000 Republican presidential primary. Coming off a big win in New Hampshire, McCain had become a threat to front-runner George W. Bush's campaign and was polling well in the next primary state, South Carolina. Which is why hundreds of Republican voters in that state received calls from a fake polling firm asking if they would still vote for Senator McCain if they knew he had fathered an illegitimate black child.

The charge was a total lie. The McCain family had a daughter who was born in Bangladesh and adopted from one of Mother Teresa's orphanages, which should have counted as a positive thing about McCain's character, but pictures of his family suddenly looked suspicious to some GOP voters. McCain lost in South Carolina, and though he won the next two states, he pulled out of the race after losing most states on Super Tuesday. Whether the calls came directly from the Bush campaign or from Bush supporters acting on their own remains unclear, and so does how much of a role the lies played in McCain's loss.

....

within the first few hours after an event. These kinds of polls are good at getting people's knee-jerk reactions, though it's important to remember—as you've probably learned in your own life— that first instincts often change once people have time to think about things a little more.

Exit polls are a little different, and they can be extremely important. Their specific purpose is to predict who will win an election, and they are conducted among voters leaving polling places, usually by news organizations. (CBS conducted the first poll of this type, during Kentucky's 1967 race for governor.) Pollsters collect data by asking a sampling of people at polling places which candidates they chose, and then they calculate early results based on those numbers. They also measure things like what voters considered the most important issues, and they include demographic information about voters.

If you've watched TV or followed online news on election night and seen networks or sites "call" races as soon as polls close or really soon afterward, that's usually because exit poll data in those races predicted that one candidate won easily. Because they go on throughout the day, exit polls collect data more quickly than actual vote counting can be done, so news organizations tend to use the polls when reporting early returns. They're not always perfectly accurate—voters can lie, or numbers can be skewed if an uneven number of one side's voters is ignored or refuses to answer—but they're generally pretty close, and responsible news organizations hold off on calling results until the exit poll data are clear.

The polls this section has covered so far are all designed to get a realistic picture of the group being sampled. Not every survey works that way. Dozens of organizations also conduct opt-in polls. Your local TV news station might ask viewers to call in and vote yes or no on a particular question. Websites have online polls that any visitor can fill in and see their results. During presidential elections, some fast-food chains even ask customers to "vote" by selecting one of two products (for example, choosing a red or blue coffee cup), and they keep track of the total as a fun promotion.

These kinds of polls are fine, and the results might be interesting, but they're not at all scientific. The people being polled are seeking to participate, whether they're choosing to click a link or to shop at a certain store. That automatically skews the make-up of the sample. Plus, people making a special effort to call into a news show and vote probably hold stronger opinions, pro or con, than the general public might.

No matter which approach they use, legitimate pollsters will identify their organization upfront when talking with voters and will never ask them for money. One of the struggles pollsters sometimes face is that voters have had bad experiences with telemarketers or other unexpected phone calls, which makes them suspicious or unwilling to participate. Another problem is that campaigns or supporters sometimes disguise themselves as pollsters to spread negative or flat-out false information about another candidate (see sidebar on page 182), which can unfairly reflect badly on real polls.

Section II
Debates

Debates are among the highest-profile parts of any major campaign. At the presidential level, they are watched by millions of people. The first Democratic debate of the 2016 cycle drew more than 15 million live viewers. The first Republican debate of the cycle was seen by 24 million. If you don't count sporting events, that debate would have broken a record at the time for the most-watched program on American cable TV. During the general election, the three debates between Hillary Clinton and Donald Trump drew a total of 259 million viewers, breaking 1992's record of 250 million. For voters who don't follow politics closely, debates (along with convention speeches) are the kinds of special events that make them tune in and help them make their choice.

Presidential debates understandably get the most attention, both in the primaries and in the general election, but debates are also common in races for the Senate and House, state offices, and local elected offices. In any election, debates are a rare opportunity to see the candidates in the same place at the same time and for them to answer questions they don't necessarily expect. The candidates aren't going to agree on "right" answers, but undecided voters can use the candidates' disagreements and how they present their ideas as the basis for choosing which of them to support.

They're such a big part of elections now that it's worth mentioning that debates are not mandatory and never have been. They are just an entrenched tradition, and not even a particularly old one.

The first fifteen presidents never had face-to-face presidential debates as candidates do now. Abraham Lincoln did have a series of famous debates with Stephen Douglas, but those took place when they faced each other in an 1858 race to represent Illinois in the Senate. (See sidebar on page 188.) The two of them ran against each other again in the presidential election two years later, but they never debated in that race.

Debates made a small comeback in the middle of the twentieth century, but they still didn't quite catch on. The 1948, 1952, and 1956 elections each included at least one debate during the primaries with candidates or their representatives, but they weren't major events like the debates we see today.

It wasn't until the 1960 race, featuring John F. Kennedy against Richard Nixon, that presidential candidates debated during the general election. They faced off four times between late September and late October, with debates held in four cities—Chicago, Washington, Los Angeles, and New York—and broadcast nationwide on all three television networks (ABC, NBC, and CBS) and on the radio. (One of the debates actually featured the candidates being filmed in different places but both responding live to the moderator's questions.)

The 1960 debates were a huge hit with Americans. The first one was watched by more than sixty-six million people. It's now historical lore that people listening on the radio thought Nixon won, but those watching on TV thought Kennedy did (partly because Nixon looked unhealthy after dealing with an illness, and he struggled with talking to the camera instead of directly to the moderators). In reality, the radio audience was a small portion; nearly 90 percent of American homes had televisions by that point, and the candidates' four debates were each watched by between 57.8 and 61 percent of households with TV. In the past, most voters never actually saw a presidential candidate campaign live unless they attended a speech; they read about them, heard them on the radio, or watched prerecorded news footage. These debates were a pretty big deal.

You might think that the success of those debates would have

THE LINCOLN-DOUGLAS DEBATES

The 1858 Illinois Senate debates between Abraham Lincoln and Stephen Douglas helped both men become political stars.

The two faced off seven times in different parts of the state, and the debate format they used is still popular in high school and college debate competitions. The "Lincoln-Douglas" format involved one candidate speaking for an hour and the other responding for ninety minutes, then the first speaker closing with another thirty. (The incumbent Douglas led off four of the seven debates.)

State legislatures still selected senators at the time, and Douglas was reelected 54–46. Still, their debates drew a lot of media coverage and raised Lincoln's profile to the point that Republican candidates in other states brought him in to campaign for them. It was in that race that Lincoln made his famous prediction that "a house divided against itself cannot stand" and that the issue of slavery was not going to be resolved without a crisis.

Even in defeat, the experience made Lincoln an obvious choice as the Republican Party's second presidential nominee, and he was

....

made future debates a no-brainer, but they didn't happen again until 1976. There were a few reasons for that, but mostly it was because the 1960 election was a special case. That race was always going to be close—only 0.2 percent of the popular vote and eighty-four electoral votes ultimately divided the two candidates—so both Nixon and Kennedy saw value in speaking before a huge national audience, and the public was extremely interested in the election. The networks also wanted to show they were civic-minded by

While Douglas won their first election face-off, Lincoln used the experience to help him dominate the rematch.

elected president just two years after the debates. He also benefited when the Democratic Party split into two factions in 1860, with Douglas running as the nominee of Northern Democrats and John Breckinridge as the Southern Democratic nominee.

broadcasting the debates, though the huge viewing numbers certainly didn't hurt.

Also, Congress actually suspended a law to allow the debate. The Communications Act of 1934 required that broadcasters give equal time to all candidates, not just those from the Republican and Democratic Parties. To make a debate between just Kennedy and Nixon legal, Congress had to temporarily suspend that law, and in 1975, the Federal Communications Commission (FCC) formally changed the rules so that debates would never need to include every party.

Presidential debates didn't happen in the next three elections, simply because one candidate refused to take part. Lyndon Johnson in 1964 was so consistently ahead in the polls that his campaign saw no reason to risk a debate, and Richard Nixon chose to avoid a repeat of his poor 1960 performance by avoiding debates in his successful 1968 and 1972 runs. In 1976 Gerald Ford and Jimmy Carter finally brought back general election debates, and they're probably not going away anytime soon.

FROM THEN TO NOW

Voters in the United States have had a chance to watch major candidates debate in every presidential race since the Ford-Carter showdown. That's just the general election. Republicans held 85 primary debates between the 1948 and 2016 cycles, and the Democrats held 104. (See sidebar on page 193.) Most of those happened from 1980 onward. As noted above, the earliest modern debates were actually between members of the same party, including a famously dull 1956 primary match (the first-ever televised debate) in which Democrats Adlai Stevenson and Estes Kefauver agreed on almost everything. Since 1976, the Democratic and Republican candidates for vice president have also held one debate in all but one election year.

While debates are now a tradition, that doesn't mean anyone has to participate. For one thing, incumbent presidents have always refused to take part in primary debates rather than make challengers seem more legitimate. In 1980 the Democratic and Republican tickets couldn't agree to terms for the vice-presidential

DEBATE ZINGERS

Debates are about policy, but they're also about candidates showing that they can think on their feet. Some of the most memorable debate lines are also pithy and funny. Here are a few examples:

"I will not make age an issue of this campaign. I am not going to exploit, for political purposes, my opponent's youth and inexperience."

> —Ronald Reagan, age seventy-three in 1984,
> when asked if he was too old to be president

"I served with Jack Kennedy. I knew Jack Kennedy. Jack Kennedy was a friend of mine. Senator, you're no Jack Kennedy."

> —Lloyd Bentsen, during the 1988 vice-presidential
> debate, when opponent Dan Quayle argued that
> he was as qualified as John F. Kennedy

"There's only three things he mentions in a sentence: a noun, and a verb, and 9/11."

> —Joe Biden, during the 2008 Democratic primary,
> making fun of Republican hopeful Rudy Giuliani

"Well, Governor, we also have fewer horses and bayonets, because the nature of our military has changed."

> —Barack Obama in 2012, when opponent
> Mitt Romney noted the United States has fewer naval
> ships than it did back when naval warfare was common

debate, so there wasn't one. Also in 1980, Republican representative John Anderson of Illinois was running as a third-party candidate, and he was polling well enough that the League of Women Voters (LWV) invited him to the first general election debate. President Jimmy Carter refused to join, so Anderson and Republican nominee Ronald Reagan debated each other. The second debate was canceled when Carter wouldn't join, but the third, between only Carter and Reagan, set a viewership record—80.6 million Americans tuned in, seeing as it was the only opportunity to watch the two of them debate.

Over the years, the ways in which presidential debates work has changed, and that's given the parties a lot more control over things.

The League of Women Voters, a genuinely nonpartisan organization, used to moderate all of the presidential debates. It hosted the early primary versions in the 1950s and ran the general election debates in 1976, 1980, and 1984. There was always some back-and-forth involved in getting candidates to agree to the rules, but the LWV decided which of their demands were reasonable.

However, in 1988 representatives from the two major parties secretly agreed on a range of demands—about everything from who could serve as moderator for the debate to how tall the candidates' podiums could be. Once the LWV found out, it withdrew as a sponsor, saying the demands "would perpetrate a fraud on the American voter."

That gave the Democratic Party and Republican Party an excuse to take over the process, forming a bipartisan (not nonpartisan) nonprofit organization called the Commission on

PRESIDENTIAL DEBATES BY THE NUMBERS

One sign of how much the public relies on debates when choosing how to vote is how popular they've become during the party primaries. Parties now hold a bunch of debates in any cycle when they don't have a president running for reelection. Here's the number of presidential debates per year, in the primary and general elections.

DEMOCRATIC PRIMARY	REPUBLICAN PRIMARY	GENERAL ELECTION
1956, 1	1948, 1 (radio only)	1960, 4
1960, 2	1980, 6	1976, 3
1968, 1	1988, 7	1980, 2
1972, 3	1996, 7	1984, 2
1976, 3	2000, 13	1988, 2
1984, 11	2008, 19	1992, 3
1988, 15	2012, 20	1996, 2
1992, 14	2016, 12	2000, 3
2000, 9		2004, 3
2004, 16		2008, 3
2008, 19		2012, 3
2016, 10		2016, 3

Presidential Debates (CPD). The CPD formally selects the venues, the moderators, and the format for presidential debates, but all those decisions really come from agreements between the parties and candidates. On one hand, the new system has meant more primary debates, so more chances for voters to see the candidates face questions. On the other, the fact that the parties run the show means they're able to avoid any surprises and the debates are quite a bit more predictable. The debates might change format slightly—a standard moderator format with the candidates at podiums, a "town hall" where they take questions (usually prescreened by the moderator) from the audience, a panel where multiple moderators ask questions, or a forum where candidates are seated at a table—but those differences are still approved by both major parties.

Also, until fairly recently, third-party candidates had a realistic chance of sharing the debate stage if they received enough support. In 1992 businessman Ross Perot was performing so well in early polls that the CPD included the third-party candidate in the three presidential debates (and his running mate, James Stockdale, in the vice-presidential one). Perot didn't win any states in November, but he won almost 19 percent of the popular vote. Because his ideas appealed to factions of both major parties, each had a plausible argument that Perot's debate performance hurt its candidate.

After that Perot experience, the two major parties decided to make it harder for anyone else to get on the stage. Rather than ban third parties, which would rightly be seen as unfair, they set the rules so that any candidate needed to average at least 15 percent in a series of polls before getting an invite. (Remember, the

FCC already got rid of the rule requiring all candidates to receive equal time.) In 1996 even Perot wasn't able to participate in any debates under the new rules. A few third-party candidates have sued the CPD over its control of the debates since then, but so far nothing has changed.

Third parties can host their own debates, too, of course. It's just hard for those debates to get on TV for a wide audience to check out, although a channel like C-SPAN might choose to air them. In 2016 Libertarian Gary Johnson and Green Party candidate Jill Stein had two televised debates, one on PBS and one on Russian news channel RT.

The two main parties also set the rules for which candidates appear on the stage during their primary debates and determine the debate schedule.

Early in the 2016 election cycle, the Republican Party had enough contenders for the nomination that it took the unusual step of hosting two back-to-back debates. The top contenders based on poll data debated during prime time, while those who missed the cut faced one another in a smaller, earlier, and less-watched debate (which earned nicknames like the kids' table or junior varsity), until enough candidates dropped out for everyone to fit on one stage. The number of primary debates has gone up since 2000, and the debates have started earlier in the election cycle. It's become normal for candidates who don't gain much support after the debates to leave the race months before anybody votes in an actual primary or caucus.

The debate formats used at the presidential level have become so popular that state and local races usually use similar ones. In races where one candidate has a big lead, it can sometimes be hard for challengers to get the front-runner to agree to a debate—someone sure they're going to win might think an unscripted debate can only hurt them. Still, most governor, Senate, and House races will have at least one debate, usually broadcast by a local news station.

Smaller races, such as for a seat in the state legislature or a mayoral race in a small town, might or might not have debates. It all comes down to whether the candidates or their parties can come to an agreement on the rules. In a city such as New York or Chicago, local news usually shows the debates for mayor. Public-access television and radio should broadcast local debates, and spectators can always watch them in person, depending on the event's ticket policies.

Section III
Fund-Raising

Say what you will about the problems with how debates work, but at least they give the candidates who qualify a more or less equal chance to get their message to voters. Campaign fund-raising is a very different case, as supporters of different candidates can raise wildly different amounts of money, which can mean more ads, more staff, and generally more chances to convince voters that they're the right choice.

When people complain about democracy being broken or special interests having too much power, this is one area they usually mention, and it's hard to argue they don't have a point. In this section, we'll focus on how fund-raising works in federal elections.

One thing members of Congress (of both parties) complain about is the amount of time they need to spend calling donors to ask for money and attending fund-raisers. How much time that takes depends on the person. A senator or representative in a close race in a big state probably needs to raise more than someone expected to win easily in a smaller territory without a pricey TV market.

Candidates for federal offices raise money from a combination of sources—individual donors, their party's national and state (and, sometimes, district and local) committees, political action committees (better known as PACs), and their own personal money.

An individual donor is any person who donates to a candidate on his or her own. As of 2020, the individual donation limit is $2,800. That number is adjusted for inflation during every election cycle. So as an individual contributor, you can only give $2,800 to any one candidate, but you could give that same amount to two or three different candidates (or more, if you're rolling in money). Also, that's the limit for the entire cycle, but it can be broken up into a few pieces. If you donated $1,800 to a candidate in the Democratic or Republican primary, you'd be able to donate another $1,000 to them during the general election.

When campaigns call to raise money, they'll say that even small donations help, and they're right, because of volume. Twenty-eight individuals donating $100 each are as valuable as one person donating the limit, and potentially more valuable, because the campaign can ask them for more money later in the cycle, while the donor who gave $2,800 is already done. Presidential candidates routinely raise millions of dollars from individual donors, so combined they're a major source of campaign cash.

Individuals can also donate: up to $5,000 per year to a PAC; $10,000 per year to party committees at the state, district, or local level ($10,000 total, not to each); and up to $35,000 per year to the national party committee. Obviously, that can add up to a level of money very few Americans can afford to give.

If you donate to a PAC or party committee, you don't get to decide which candidates get the money. For example, both the Democrats and Republicans have campaign committees that focus on House races (the Democratic Congressional Campaign Committee and the National Republican Congressional Committee, respectively). They send money to the House races where the committee leaders think their candidates need the most help, or where they think extra money can make the biggest difference. There are also limits on how much any PAC or party committee can contribute to any one candidate (with $5,000 per election at the high end).

As you might guess, those numbers are still small compared to the kind of big money that's sometimes spent on elections. That's where outside funding groups come in.

GROUPS FROM THE OUTSIDE

Other groups that spend significantly on elections include 527 groups, Super PACs, and 501(c)(4) organizations. Both numbered terms come from the section of the federal tax code that applies to them. The money these groups raise and spend can play a big role, so it's worth understanding how they work.

A 527 group is defined as a tax-exempt political organization. That includes party groups such as the Republican National Committee and Democratic National Committee. It also includes

"Politics has got so expensive that it takes lots of money to even get beat with nowadays."

**—COMEDIAN, ACTOR, AND POLITICAL SATIRIST WILL ROGERS IN 1931.
IF HE THOUGHT THINGS WERE EXPENSIVE THEN . . .**

committees that handle election activity for well-known advocacy organizations such as the Sierra Club, EMILY'S List, and the Club for Growth. Those kinds of advocacy organizations run campaign ads about particular issues relevant to what they do, but they don't specifically tell voters which candidate the organization wants them to choose ("Vote for lower taxes," not "Vote for this guy"). Those kinds of 527 groups have been around for ages. As long as they play by the rules, and their ads never expressly say how to vote, they can raise unlimited money and can take contributions from anyone.

In 2002 Congress passed the Bipartisan Campaign Reform Act (also called McCain-Feingold, after its cocreators). It introduced many reforms, most notably banning corporations or unions from broadcasting campaign ads in the last sixty days before an election (more on that shortly). But it didn't change how 527s work, so a new kind of 527 organization started popping up during the 2004 election cycle, formed specifically to influence that election. One famous example was the group called Swift Boat Veterans and POWs for Truth, which ran misleading attack ads about Democratic nominee John Kerry and the medals he won in Vietnam, but never specifically told voters not to vote for him or to choose his opponent. A minor technicality, but one that made the ads legal. Other new 527 groups like America Coming Together and the Media Fund didn't get as much attention, but similarly spent millions on that election.

Any 527s still need to disclose who donated to them, register with the Internal Revenue Service (IRS), and follow rules about their advocacy. Many reformers called for changes to the 527 rules after the 2004 election, but those organizations were soon replaced as campaign finance reformers' biggest challenge.

One of the most important recent Supreme Court cases, the 2010 decision in *Citizens United vs. Federal Election Commission* (often referred to as simply *Citizens United*) fundamentally altered how campaign finance in the United States works. The ruling eliminated the ban on corporations and unions paying for electioneering communications and independent expenditures. Those organizations still can't give money directly to a candidate for federal office, but they can now spend unlimited money pushing for any candidate's victory or defeat. Another 2010 case that used *Citizens United* as a legal precedent, *SpeechNow.org v. FEC*, ruled that there's no limit on how much anyone can donate to independent-expenditure groups. Combined, those two cases meant any entity—a wealthy person, a corporation, you name it—can donate as much money as they want to groups working outside the campaigns to influence the outcome.

Those two rulings led to the 2012 rise of expenditure-only committees, better known as Super PACs. Unlike regular PACs, Super PACs can't donate directly to candidates, since that would violate the ban on corporations and unions donating directly. Unlike 527s, however, they *can* support specific candidates. Many of the largest Super PACs exist for only one election cycle and only to support or oppose one candidate (there are a few exceptions, such as FreedomWorks for America and House Majority PAC). They're not allowed to coordinate their efforts with campaigns or parties, but the rules around that come with a lot of loopholes. After all, it's easy enough for a Super PAC to figure out what a candidate wants from public speeches and interviews with the candidate or his or her campaign staff. If someone lets it be known publicly that they liked or didn't like an ad the Super PAC ran, it's easy for the Super PAC to react to that, without the two sides ever officially interacting.

Even Super PACs need to disclose where they get their money, though, so people looking to hide their influence can instead donate to 501(c)(4) groups.

On the one hand, 501(c)(4) groups are defined as nonprofit social welfare organizations. They can get involved with politics, as long as that isn't their primary purpose (for example, they can't spend more than half of their money on political activities). Historically, that applied to groups like local civics leagues, as well as organizations such as the American Civil Liberties Union (ACLU) and the American Association of Retired Persons (AARP). But after the 2010 court rulings, the IRS was flooded with applications from new groups wanting to be defined as 501(c)(4)s. Many of these groups are essentially nonprofit PACs that operate independently of the parties and campaigns, but can raise and spend unlimited money without having to disclose their donors. According to the Center for Responsive Politics, these nonprofits spent even more than Super PACs in the 2010 election cycle, by about a three-to-two ratio.

THE IMPACT

These recent changes to the campaign finance system have been controversial for several reasons. For one, they make the process less democratic, as one rich individual or corporation can donate unlimited money and can make candidates at least appear to answer to those individuals. They've made the cost of elections, which already grew every cycle, grow even faster. Advertising is one of any campaign's biggest expenses, and outside groups picking up the tab for much of it (even unofficially) has an impact on how candidates and parties raise and spend money.

Ads from outside groups can also be particularly nasty, since the candidate they support doesn't have to take responsibility for them. And when ads come from groups that don't need to disclose their donors at all, voters never find out who's behind the messages they're seeing. If, for example, a company that pollutes near a town is running ads trying to take out the member of Congress attempting to make it pay for the cleanup, voters should at least have the ability to know where those ads are coming from and consider that when voting. These rulings mean they don't always get to find out.

By the 2012 election, the impact of these changes was already pretty obvious in terms of the big money in the race. The total spending on the presidential race from outside groups more than doubled between 2008 and 2012, making it the first cycle measured in billions instead of millions, and that number increased in 2016 (see sidebar on page 203). Even that understates the situation, because the 2008 election had two primary processes with several viable candidates, and in 2012 only the Republican primaries were contested.

It's not just the presidential race. In 2014 the most expensive Senate race was in North Carolina, where Republican Thom Tillis defeated Democratic incumbent Kay Hagan. More than $118 million was spent on that seat in the general election, but only about $35 million of that was spent by the two candidates' campaigns, with the rest coming from outside groups. On the House side, 2014's priciest race was in California's seventh district, where Democratic incumbent Ami Bera spent about $4.4 million in victory, Republican challenger Doug Ose spent about $5.1 million in the loss, and outside groups spent about $13.7 million.

In total, the 2018 midterms cost about 35 percent more than the 2014 edition, and outside spending was up 61 percent. The

2018 race for Georgia's sixth district between Karen Handel and Lucy McBath cost more than twice as much as that California race between Bera and Ose.

If you watch broadcast television in the last few weeks before a general election, you can't help seeing dozens and dozens of political ads. Thanks to the Bipartisan Campaign Reform Act, since 2002, politicians appear in any ad that comes directly from the campaign, to give it an official endorsement (as ordered in part of the law known as the "stand by your ad" provision). If the ad features audio or video, the candidate will say something along the lines of, "I'm Joe Candidate, and I approve this message." Ads from outside groups might or might not feel like they were approved by the candidate, but that distinction can be lost on voters who don't know about or don't fully understand how campaign-finance laws have changed in a short amount of time.

Section IV
Ballot Measures

Most laws are passed by Congress or by its state and local doppel-gangers. However, some states allow a certain amount of direct democracy in the form of ballot measures, meaning voters on Election Day also need to choose whether the proposals on the ballot become law.

These measures only apply to state and local, not federal, law, and each state has its own rules for whether ballot measures are allowed and how they work. The idea of ballot measures in the United States goes back to just after the founding, when Georgia included the concept in its state constitution. However, the modern process really began during the Progressive Era of the late nineteenth century and early twentieth century as one of many reforms aimed at helping the people serve as a check on the government. Today, some states heavily rely on them, while others use ballot measures only in special circumstances.

There are three main types of ballot measures in the United States.

Legislative referendum, also called legislative referral, means the state legislature makes the decision to put a proposed law up to a public vote. Sometimes it's mandatory, as when an amendment to the state constitution is being proposed—every state except Delaware requires that voters get to weigh in on any constitutional amendment, as a reasonable check on the state legislature's power. It's also common with laws that involve bond issues, because citizens will need to pay taxes to fund a project, and this way they have a say in whether they'll spend that money.

A second type of ballot measure, popular referendum, means voters are trying to repeal a specific law passed by the state legislature. This is sometimes called a *citizens' veto*, and that's a pretty good description for it. More than twenty states allow this kind of measure, and petitioners need to get a minimum number of valid signatures before the referendum qualifies for the ballot. That number is different from state to state.

The third, and most popular, variety is the ballot initiative. In the states that allow initiatives—as of 2018, twenty-four plus the District of Columbia—any citizen or organization can write a measure and have it appear on the ballot. The initiative still needs to meet certain state-specific requirements, and it always needs a minimum number of signatures before appearing on the ballot—a way to demonstrate the measure has enough support to justify having voters weigh in on it.

WHAT THEY'VE DONE

Well more than half of the ballot initiatives in the United States have come from only six states—Arizona, California, Colorado, North Dakota, Oregon, and Washington—so they're clearly more popular in the West.

California is particularly fond of ballot initiatives, so we'll use it as an example. Since 2000, every even-year election has seen between six and eighteen statewide initiatives for voters to consider, plus any number of local measures. For many years, voters even received booklets not much smaller than an old-fashioned phone book that included the wording of every initiative and arguments for and against each. In 2011 California governor Jerry Brown signed a law passed by the state legislature that made an important change to the process. Rather than appear on a ballot in any election (including off-year primaries), initiatives would only appear during general elections in November, when turnout is higher and more voters would decide every ballot entry's fate.

To continue with the California example, here's just some of what voters there did via statewide ballot initiatives during the 2012 election alone. They agreed to increase sales and use taxes by one quarter of one cent for a four-year period and increase income taxes for seven years on anybody making more than a quarter of a million dollars per year, with the money going to education. They voted in favor of congressional redistricting being handled by a nonpartisan commission. They supported a change to term-limit laws for the state legislature, limiting legislators to twelve years combined in either body (instead of the old system, with separate limits for the state's two houses). They voted to increase prison sentences for anyone convicted of human trafficking and to make convicted traffickers register as sex offenders.

They even voted for an initiative that changed an earlier voter-passed initiative. In 1994 California voters had passed a "three strikes" law, which won with 72 percent of the vote and meant that anyone convicted of three felonies was subject to life in prison. That law had its share of unintended consequences, as many nonviolent criminals were subject to the same life sentences as murderers and rapists. In 2012 voters passed a modification to the three strikes rule, so that only violent offenders would receive life sentences, and people already serving life for their personal drug use or other less-serious crimes were able to appeal.

Overall, that year the same voters passed six initiatives and rejected seven, so it's not as if getting a measure on the ballot guarantees success. Among the things California voters rejected that year: a statewide ban on the death penalty; a ban on corporate and union contributions to state candidates; and the mandatory labeling of genetically modified food. In the latter case, agribusiness company Monsanto (for which genetically modified food is a big part of business) and other companies spent an estimated $46 million campaigning against the ballot initiative.

Even though initiatives only directly affect the state where they're passed, they can impact other states too. If a measure passes and it winds up working well for one state, voters and legislators elsewhere are more likely to try the same idea in their state.

TAKING INITIATIVE

Ballot initiatives don't always originate at the grassroots level, but they can definitely show how quickly public opinion changes on certain issues.

In 2003 Massachusetts became the first state to legalize marriage for gay and lesbian citizens. However, the idea of marriage equality was much less popular nationwide than it would become within just a few years, particularly among Republicans. President George W. Bush opposed marriage equality, and his 2004 campaign saw an opportunity to increase turnout among its voters. A concerted effort by Republicans in eleven states put the marriage issue on the ballot, in the form of eleven proposed amendments to state constitutions, each requiring marriage to apply only to heterosexual couples.

The plan worked—voters in all eleven states supported the measure, and in nine did so with more than 60 percent of the vote ("blue" states Oregon and Michigan were the exceptions). It also helped Republican turnout in the crucial swing state of Ohio, and in Kentucky, where it might have helped decide a close Senate race.

Just a few years later, that victory would have seemed impossible. Several state legislatures legalized marriage equality, and voters in four states used a 2012 round of ballot initiatives to endorse it. In the summer of 2015, the Supreme Court settled the issue by requiring all states to issue marriage licenses for same-sex couples (see page 49).

The legalization of marijuana is another example of how ballot measures have changed the law in a short span of time, with lots of funding and interest coming in from all over the country.

In 2012, 55.3 percent of Colorado voters and 55.7 of voters in the state of Washington backed ballot initiatives to legalize and regulate (and tax) small amounts of the drug for people

Progress can happen at the ballot box. In less than a decade, voters went from approving bans on marriage equality to supporting the right to marry.

twenty-one and over, making them the first states to legalize pot for nonmedical use. That meant two states were still in violation of federal drug laws, but the US Department of Justice chose not to enforce marijuana laws in those states, allowing the new state laws to stand.

Alaska, Oregon, and the District of Columbia were next to legalize the drug. In 2016 nine states had marijuana legalization on the ballot, and it passed in eight (four for recreational pot, and four for medical use only). Three more states legalized it via 2018 midterm ballot initiatives (one recreational, two medical). The victories on the ballot have prompted several members of Congress to introduce bills calling for federal legalization, which would have been pretty unlikely without the outcomes in Colorado and Washington.

The federal government has also been known to adopt ideas that have already been proven to work at the state level. As the Monsanto example shows, state initiatives can have huge political stakes, with one side trying to stop an idea from spreading, and the other trying to establish a model that others can copy. (For more examples, see sidebar on page 208.) Because of that, campaigns for and against some ballot measures can feel a bit like campaigns for and against candidates, with everything from negative advertising to huge get-out-the-vote efforts.

Ballot measures seem like a true example of democracy, and they can be. Or they can be ways for special interests to get around the legislative process. Once again, they're a tool that can be used for good or bad, depending on your perspective.

Getting a measure on the ballot is also one of the easiest ways for young people to get more involved in the political process. In the next (and final) chapter, we'll talk about some of the other ways, beyond simply voting, that you can play a part in politics, during an election or any other time. ■

CHAPTER 6

MORE WAYS TO GET INVOLVED

A few chapters back, we focused on what you personally should do when it comes to voting, and that's obviously a good starting point for getting involved in politics. It's relatively easy. It costs you basically nothing but time and doesn't take up all that much of it. Even with primaries and special elections, voting itself is a commitment of only a few hours per year.

For those of you who want to do more, or aren't yet old enough to vote, there are heaps of roles that young Americans can play in campaigns and elections. You might decide that politics is something that interests you as a career, and some early volunteer experience can be a big help in getting a first job in the field. Or you might just want to help a particular candidate who shares your ideals and can use all the help he or she can get. Or you might care most about a particular issue and want to do what you can to change policy around it, whether it's a cause as large-scale as fighting discrimination or protecting the environment, or as local as building a new public library or providing more adult education classes in the community.

As involved (or uninvolved) as you want to be, you can be. You could do something as simple as wearing a T-shirt with the candidate's name and putting a campaign sign on your lawn, or you might opt for a months-long, full-time campaign job. These are just a few of the ways you can play a role before, during, and after Election Day.

Section I
Volunteering without a Candidate or a Campaign

We'll cover volunteering with a campaign shortly, but you can also help out without needing to take sides.

Voter registration drives, which we mentioned earlier, can always use volunteers. Organizations including the LWV, Rock the Vote, Voto Latino, and hundreds of others work to get people signed up to vote. So do political parties and campaigns. If you want to help with registration, there's no shortage of options. Many of these organizations—more than four thousand in 2018—take part in National Voter Registration Day, which is pretty much what it sounds like. Held on the fourth Tuesday of September, it's an annual event that started in 2012, with the goal of registering as many Americans to vote as possible. The day of activism started in response to estimates that during the 2008 election, some six million Americans wanted to vote but missed the registration deadline. It's a good event and it raises visibility, but registering voters continues all the way up to each state's deadline. That means you can help out on your own schedule.

If working with an organization isn't your thing, you can also just start your own, small-scale voter registration drive. Post offices and other government buildings—pretty much any of the offices covered by the Motor Voter law—will have extra registration forms on hand, which you can use to sign up your family, friends, and anybody else. As with any registrations, they'll only count if you get the forms to your local election office before your state's deadline. Voter registration is a never-ending need. With midterms and off-years, there's always another election coming up (the schedule we covered in chapter 2), and there are always people turning eighteen or relocating, so voter registration is the kind of volunteer opportunity that you can do consistently for years if you want to, or you can just help out one time.

Another nonpartisan way to get involved is to serve as a poll worker on Election Day. Every polling place needs people to greet and check in voters, give them their ballots, answer questions, and make sure that the completed ballots are filed correctly. Some polling places also use poll monitors, whose job is specifically to keep an eye out for voter fraud (such as people trying to vote more than once or using someone else's ID) or voter intimidation (such as people campaigning too close to the polling place or trying to scare away voters).

Volunteers in these roles usually need to be registered to vote at the same polling place where they're working, though, depending on the state, there can be specific exceptions for college students who are registered somewhere else. Some election offices require that workers include a mix of registered Democrats and registered Republicans, out of a concern that both parties need to keep an eye on each other.

Poll workers go through training before Election Day, which typically takes just a few hours. As you probably figured, the actual workday can be a long one, since volunteers need to show up early enough to set up and be ready before the first voters arrive, and they stay after polls close to make sure all of the ballots are properly processed. (All but the most merciless of polling places will have coffee on hand.) In some places, once again on a state-by-state basis, poll workers actually take home a small amount of pay for their time that day and for the time they spend training for the gig. The states that have early voting have even more need for poll workers, since there are more shifts to fill, though the early voting days might have shorter hours.

The US Election Assistance Commission—the office created by the Help America Vote Act in 2002—has links to state-by-state requirements for poll workers on its website, EAC.gov.

Section II
Volunteer or Work for a Campaign

Campaigns are constantly looking for volunteers. Why not? It's free help, and candidates and parties in the midst of a campaign are almost always happy to have it. Sometimes, they'll even have paid positions available for local roles, depending on the campaign's needs and budget (and depending on your level of work experience). On your end, working or volunteering with a campaign is a good chance to learn more about the process behind the scenes and to help a particular candidate. It looks good on a résumé and is a good way to find out if politics is something that interests you as a career. Plus, if you like the people you work with, it can be a lot of fun.

First, and this should go without saying, find a candidate you really want to help. If you're going to put in a lot of hours and hard work, it should be for a goal you care about achieving, not just backing whoever you think has the best chance of winning or taking the first opportunity that comes up. This way, if the campaign wins, it's going to be more exciting if you feel like you accomplished something positive. If it loses, you'll look back and at least feel as though you honestly tried to do that.

Also, think about what you want out of a volunteer opportunity. On a presidential campaign, you'll get to work with a lot more people, but you probably won't have as big of a role. On a local campaign, you have a better chance of getting more responsibility and learning a wider variety of skills. One approach isn't necessarily better; it just depends on what you want.

So what kinds of tasks might you handle as a campaign volunteer or worker? Here are a few examples.

BALLOT ACCESS

Every state has a minimum number of valid signatures that are required before a candidate can even appear on the ballot. It varies by office, too; someone running for president needs more signatures than someone running for one House district. In some states, party nominees appear on the ballot automatically, as long as the party met certain voting thresholds last time around, while other states still require signatures for everyone.

Signatures are usually collected by volunteers in the same kinds of places where you'll probably see voter registration drives. Just like the ones for voter registration, signatures for ballot access are then sent to a state election office, which verifies whether the signatures are valid. If enough of them check out, the candidate's name will show up on the ballot. Anyone trying to obtain ballot access needs to make sure his or her supporters turn in at least 20 percent more signatures than the actual target number, because some won't be valid—people give fake names, don't live in the same state or district, sign up with an address that can't be verified, or write illegibly.

WRITING IN A WINNER

If candidates don't achieve ballot access, their only choice (other than giving up) is to run as a write-in candidate, which is pretty much what it sounds like—voters need to write in the candidate's name on their ballot. It's always a challenge to get enough voters to take that extra step and vote for someone whose name isn't listed.

It's a challenge, but it's not impossible. Most write-ins win at the local level, which makes sense, because fewer voters need to write them in and the candidates have an easier time meeting a large percentage of potential voters. Quite a few state officials and several members of the House of Representatives were elected this way.

Even three US senators have won their seats as write-ins: William Knowland in California in 1946, Strom Thurmond in South Carolina in 1954, and Lisa Murkowski in Alaska in 2010. In Murkowski's case, she was an incumbent senator at the time but lost the Republican

If candidates fail to hit the minimum number, their only shot is to run as a write-in candidate (see sidebar above).

Ballot access is one area in which the two-party system sometimes creates rules designed to keep the two parties in power. State governments tend to pick signature numbers high enough that someone with the backing of a major party can hit them easily, but an independent might need serious help. That's not unusual in primaries either, as underdog candidates in both the Democratic and Republican Parties also sometimes fall short of ballot access in some states, if they don't have enough supporters to get them past that hurdle. Even if a candidate is polling well

primary to far-right candidate Joe Miller (an example of the primary-as-a-verb trend we discussed in chapter 2). In that case, the state's Supreme Court ruled that polling places should have a list of write-in candidates for voters to look at—something Murkowski had requested, given that her last name wasn't the easiest one to spell correctly.

Spelling matters, too, and each state has its own rules about how close voters need to get to the right letters for a write-in to count. In the 2010 Alaska example, Miller challenged a number of the write-in votes, but Murkowski defeated both Miller and the Democratic nominee by a big enough margin that those challenges didn't matter. In Thurmond's case, his campaign gave out pencils with his name on them at events, so voters could see how to spell it correctly.

....

in early states, not being on the ballot in a few of them can kill an underdog's campaign.

Signing a petition to allow someone access to the ballot isn't the same thing as supporting them; you're just helping to give voters another option to choose from. (Tip: That's a good thing to point out to people when you're out there looking for signatures.) For many elections, you can sign petitions for every would-be candidate in every party, both in the primary and in the general election. (There are some exceptions, such as the Chicago mayoral election. As always, check your state and local rules.)

Also, ballot access applies to the kinds of referenda and ballot measures we covered in the last chapter. If you'd rather work to get a particular issue on the ballot instead of a particular candidate, that's always an option. Or you can do both, though that usually means working with separate organizations.

GETTING THE WORD OUT

One of the most important jobs that campaign workers and volunteers do is letting people know about candidates and their positions.

Obviously, a lot of that is the candidate's job, between campaign speeches, debates, and advertisements. But one person only has so much time. Candidates also rely on their supporters to spread the message through *canvassing*.

When most people think of canvassing, they probably picture going door to door and talking to people about the campaign, or talking to passersby in popular areas. ("Door to door" doesn't always mean every door; campaigns often have lists of specific addresses to visit.) Volunteers might canvass alone, or in pairs or small groups. If you're starting out, you might be paired with a more experienced campaign worker who can show you what to do.

Typically, volunteers have a few key talking points to bring up with any voter who opens the door and is willing to discuss the election. Usually, that means letting voters know who the candidate is and what office they're seeking, giving an overview of their platform, and explaining when the election will be held. Volunteers also usually carry campaign brochures or other literature that they can give to voters or leave at residences where nobody's home (on a doorknob or porch is fine, but not in a mailbox; that's illegal).

Honestly, not every interaction with a potential voter is going to be fun. As you can imagine, not everyone wants to talk about politics. And you'll run into some people who support a different candidate or a different political perspective and will feel the need to tell you all about it. A certain number of them will treat political disagreement as an excuse to be obnoxious, or even hostile. But others will actually want to talk and learn more. In some cases, you'll get to educate voters about issues, introduce them to a candidate they've never heard about but might actually like, or even just let existing supporters know when to vote and what they can do to help. In some cases, you might help undecided voters make up their minds or even change their minds about who to support. In a local election, it might only take a few voters switching from one candidate to another to change the outcome of the race.

Another approach is *phone banking*, which is basically the same thing as canvassing but done by phone. You might make the calls from a campaign headquarters or your home, and the conversation is similar to the in-person version. The advantage is that you can contact more people in a shift than you could by going door to door, and you can easily avoid confrontations. The disadvantage is it might not be as thorough or convincing as a good in-person chat.

"Raising awareness" might sound like a buzzword concept, but the biggest challenge many candidates face is that voters who don't closely follow politics don't even know which candidates are running for office. It can be easy for people who pay attention and know what's going on to forget that many Americans don't. (Remember that a whole lot of Americans can't even name the vice president.) For candidates in races that don't get a lot of media attention and candidates who can't afford a lot of advertising, canvassing is often the best way to let voters know about them. You might also get voters to put up a yard or window sign, letting even more people know about the campaign. (Tip: Don't put signs on people's property without their okay. It's rude and also gives them a reason to dislike your candidate.)

Canvassing is a good way to inform voters, and it also has a research function for the campaign. By talking to people, either face-to-face or on the phone, campaign staffers can learn who is likely to vote for their candidate. Canvassers can encourage supporters to sign up for an e-mail or snail mail list to get more information during the course of the campaign, and those lists are used when asking for donations, seeking additional volunteers, or organizing get-out-the-vote efforts.

In a presidential campaign, canvassing volunteers might travel from state to state (or at least call voters in different states), depending on which states are coming up in the primary schedule or which are considered swing states in that election (see page 68). If you volunteer with a political party rather than a candidate, you might go to other House districts in your own state or even visit different states for a range of races, as your schedule allows.

OTHER WAYS TO HELP

Those are some of the larger-scale efforts where volunteers and new workers tend to help the most, but there are other options.

You can organize events for supporters of the candidate or issue you back. Maybe it's getting local supporters together to watch a debate, hosting a weekly meet-up at a coffee shop to talk about the campaign, or putting together a student group at a high school or a college.

Donating money is another option. As we discussed in the last chapter, campaigns that don't rely on big donors need help from their grassroots supporters. There are, of course, limits to how much an individual can contribute directly to a campaign, but any donation will be appreciated. You can also donate by buying campaign gear such as T-shirts and bumper stickers, which contributes a few bucks to the campaign and advertises for it anytime you go out wearing or displaying your purchase. (Some of the gear also looks cool.) Campaigns always need volunteers to help raise money, whether by calling supporters or staffing fund-raisers.

Speaking of staffing, campaigns also need logistical support. If a campaign is hosting any kind of event, it might need volunteers to do anything from checking in people to setting up chairs to passing out snacks. If you have a car, you can drive volunteers around or even drive the candidate around when he or she is in town. And when the candidate is giving a speech, campaigns may want volunteers to attend (particularly young volunteers), both to increase attendance and to have an enthusiastic reaction from supporters.

Of course, Election Day itself is a huge volunteer opportunity. You can talk to voters and hand out literature outside of polling places, as long as you stand far enough away from the actual polls. You can help with get-out-the-vote efforts, calling or texting supporters to remind them to vote and to make sure they know the location of their local polling place. There might be opportunities to drive voters to the polls or to do some last-minute campaigning in public places.

You can help out around the campaign office too. Even if you only have a free day here and there, you can help with data entry, answering phones, greeting people, stuffing letters into envelopes, and any number of other office tasks.

A PAIR OF FAMOUS CAMPAIGN WORKERS

If politics is something you might want to do for a living, early campaign experience can be a big help. Just ask the Clintons.

Bill and the future Hillary Clinton (Hillary Rodham at the time) worked on George McGovern's 1972 presidential campaign. The couple, who were both in law school at Yale, took a break from their studies for a few months and moved to Texas, where Bill co-ran the campaign in the state and Hillary worked on voter registration in Austin and San Antonio.

Senator McGovern lost to incumbent president Richard Nixon in a landslide, but the Clintons made lifelong political allies on the campaign; many of their 1972 coworkers worked on or volunteered for one or both of the Clintons' future presidential campaigns.

The Clintons aren't alone in having worked on other campaigns before their own political careers got underway. Before he was an elected official, George W. Bush worked on a successful 1988 presidential campaign, but he had an obvious in—the candidate who hired him was his dad. Barack Obama didn't work for a specific candidate, but he worked on political issues as a community

As technology advances, young people who grew up with it and can use it effectively are extremely valuable to campaigns. Barack Obama's 2008 and 2012 campaigns were good examples of the impact volunteers can have. A record 2.2 million volunteers took part, including many students and recent grads, and the campaign actively used e-mail and social media to talk to supporters at every stage of the race. That's something all presi-

Bill Clinton is a practicing lawyer who has taught law at the University of Arkansas at Fayetteville and at the University of Arkansas at Little Rock, where he taught criminal justice to students and law enforcement officers. In 1976 he was elected Arkansas attorney general and two years later, he was elected governor.

Clinton was born in Hope, Arkansas and grew up in Hot Springs, where he attended the public schools. He, his wife Hillary and their two-year old daughter, Chelsea, reside in Little Rock. He is a member of the Immanuel Baptist Church.

Bill Clinton will work to create more jobs, keep the jobs we have and help Arkansans train for better jobs. But he can't do these things without your help. He needs your support, your contributions and your vote.
Put Bill Clinton in the Governor's Office.
Vote for Bill Clinton, Governor For Arkansas.

CLINTON
GOVERNOR

Paid for by the Clinton For Governor Committee.
Jimmie Red Jones, Chairman, George Kell, Treasurer.

organizer in Chicago before running for office himself. There are dozens of examples. The McGovern campaign manager the Clintons worked for was Gary Hart, who later ran for the Democratic presidential nomination in the 1984 and 1988 primaries.

Just six years after working on the McGovern campaign, Bill Clinton was working on his own run for governor of Arkansas.

dential campaigns (and most campaigns in general) now do at least pretty well, and they may have opportunities to help with social media, letter writing, or other communications roles.

HOW TO SIGN UP

Once you have an idea about what you want to do, your best bet is to contact a campaign directly. Any candidate running for office should have a campaign website with contact information, and the site should have a specific area with information for potential volunteers. One important note: If the candidate you're contacting is already in an elected office—whether they're running for reelection or seeking an office higher than the one they already hold—make sure to contact their campaign office, not the office for their current job. There are rules requiring a separation between campaign activities and governing activities, and there will be different staff members working on each.

If you want to work for one party on multiple campaigns, get in touch with your state or local party office. Tell them you want to volunteer, what kind of campaign you want to help, and what kind of role you're seeking. You can write, call, or just show up at your local party office and talk to someone. While candidates and parties need volunteers, there are also lots of people looking to get involved, so talking to someone directly can be a better way to get real work to do than just filling out an e-mail form. It makes sure somebody knows your name and either your face or voice.

The bottom line is that whatever you want to do and whatever skills you have, there's probably a way for you to help a candidate or a party of your choice.

Section III
Activism Outside of a Political Campaign

Maybe you want to get involved in politics, but you don't want to work for any particular candidate or party. That's cool. It doesn't prevent you from taking part in the process. If there is a particular issue you really care about (or more than one), you can volunteer to help that cause.

Unless your chosen issue is obscure, your challenge will be having too many choices rather than too few. If, for example, preserving the environment is your main interest, you could work with Greenpeace, the National Resources Defense Council, Defenders of Wildlife, Friends of the Earth, 350.org, Earthjustice, or any number of other valuable organizations. It's easy to make a similar list if you want to work on issues around gender equality, racial equality, poverty, tax policy, healthcare policy, animal rights, foreign policy, gun control, reproductive rights, farm policy . . . choose an issue, and you'll have your pick of players.

In many cases, grassroots organizations—the term *grassroots* comes from the idea that the movement grows from the ground up—use volunteers (and a smaller number of paid workers) in a way similar to campaigns. A lot of the same roles described in the last section can also be performed for an issue-based group. Canvassing (once again, either in person or by phone) is a popular example, either to raise awareness about an issue or to ask for donations. You can donate money, attend events, collect signatures for a petition to the government, work in a regional office, and many of the other things you would do for an election campaign.

Lobbying is another form of activism. The word *lobbying* often (and understandably) gets a bad rap because Washington, DC, is full of professional lobbyists who make a lot of money. By 2011, professional lobbyists had earned more than $3 billion combined, and a few thousand registered lobbyists focused just on healthcare policy alone. They're effective at getting meetings with elected officials, and they work full-time on advocating their positions.

STUDENTS HAVING THEIR SAY

On February 14, 2018, a former student brought a semiautomatic rifle to Marjory Stoneman Douglas High School in Parkland, Florida. In only about six minutes, he murdered fourteen students and three staff members and wounded another seventeen people. Unfortunately, shootings like this had become frighteningly common in the United States; since 2013, students at more than three hundred schools had endured one.

The uncommon part of this event was the role surviving students played after the shooting, leading nationwide efforts to toughen gun laws. Organizing via social media (with the influential #NeverAgain hashtag), appearing on talk shows, writing for publications, and

....

(A similar situation is probably true in your state capital; it isn't specifically a federal situation.)

For the record, quite a few lobbyists advocate for causes they genuinely support, but there's also a less-than-ideal revolving door of former members of Congress becoming high-paid lobbyists and pushing their old colleagues to get certain things done. For more than 150 years, professional lobbyists have been required to register, because their ability to influence policy was significant enough that the government decided people should at least know who was talking to public officials and on behalf of which special interests.

That doesn't make lobbying automatically bad. It's protected by the First Amendment, as part of the right to petition the government, and it isn't limited to professionals. Issue-focused orga-

contacting their representatives, the students helped keep gun control in the national conversation. Most impressively, on March 24, 2018, they organized the March for Our Lives—a student-led demonstration that brought hundreds of thousands of people to Washington and inspired hundreds of other rallies around the country. The March for Our Lives was the largest student protest since the Vietnam War, and the student leaders have continued to speak out—trying to encourage politicians to support safety measures such as background checks and limits on certain weapons, urging young voters to hold those politicians accountable, and helping flip some congressional seats in 2018.

....

nizations sometimes travel to Washington or to state capitals to lobby representatives about pending legislation or issues that members feel aren't receiving enough attention. You can take part in those kinds of efforts, meeting with representatives to talk about policy. Also, lobbying doesn't need to focus on elected officials. Holding informational events in the community or writing about an issue are ways to influence public opinion, and getting people to care about something can be an important step in encouraging elected officials to pay attention.

Protests are always an option too. Grassroots groups have used protesting as a technique since before the United States was even a country. After all, a series of protests in Boston was one of the ways that colonists complained to the government (in that case, back in London) in an effort to change its policies. Probably the most famous example was the Boston Tea Party in 1773, when a group called the Sons of Liberty dumped British tea into Boston Harbor, protesting a policy that flooded the American market with cheap tea and gave one British company a monopoly on the beverage.

Throughout American history, protests have been an important way for people to gain attention for important issues, win support, and get enough people involved that the government has to do something. The labor movement, the civil rights movement, the women's suffrage movement, the anti-war movement during the invasion of Vietnam—there are dozens of examples of people and organizations outside government getting together and making their voices heard. Martin Luther King Jr.'s peaceful 1963 March on Washington for Jobs and Freedom, the one during which he gave his famous "I Have a Dream" speech, drew about a quarter of a million people.

Protests don't always get results—hundreds of thousands (possibly millions) of Americans protested against the invasion of Iraq in 2003, and it happened anyway. But on the overall scorecard, protests have helped Americans get equal voting rights, cleaner air and water, a forty-hour workweek and job safety, and many, many other things people often take for granted. Those are definitely big examples, but smaller protests at the city or town level—whether specifically about a local issue or as part of a bigger movement—can be extremely effective.

Marches and demonstrations are only one form of protest. You might take part in an organized boycott of a business that supports policies you dislike, and larger activist organizations might have the numbers to pull that off. Sometimes, the combination of lost business and bad publicity will urge companies to change their ways. Individual companies have ceased relying on child labor, stopped using certain ingredients in food, or improved conditions for workers based on activist-led boycotts.

Depending on what causes you support and what organizations you join, activism can take very different forms, and it can be an effective way to change government policy from outside the system.

Section IV
Run for Office

Of course, you're not limited to deciding which candidate would be the best for a certain job. If it's something that interests you, there's no reason not to run for office yourself.

To run for the House of Representatives, you only need to be twenty-five, and it's only thirty for the Senate. Former vice president Joe Biden, for example, won his first Senate election at twenty-nine, as he turned thirty before actually taking office. In 2018 Alexandria Ocasio-Cortez of New York became the youngest woman ever elected to the House, at twenty-nine. For state or local offices, you can be even younger than that. How young, of course, depends on state and local election law; eighteen tends to be a common minimum age.

Obviously, the smaller the race, the better your chances of winning. Small towns have elected mayors in their late teens and early twenties, from time to time, for decades. (See sidebar on page 230 for a few examples.) Government boards, such as city councils and school boards, are also popular targets for young,

A FEW YOUNG LEADERS

In case you think young candidates are always long shots, here are just a few examples of citizens who ran for mayor and won. In these cases, the mayor was too young to legally buy a beer in some parts of the country but old enough to win an election.

In 1993 Kevin Tripp was elected mayor of South Renovo, Pennsylvania, when he was only nineteen. The town had a hard time finding candidates for the gig, and Tripp won as a write-in. In 2011 eighteen-year-old Jeremy Minnier became mayor of Aredale, Iowa, tripling the vote total of the small town's incumbent mayor. (How small? He won 24–8.) Christopher Portman not only won the general election for mayor of Mercer, Pennsylvania, in 2001, but he won both the Republican and Democratic primaries in the process. (Eighteen when elected, he took office at nineteen, but served only part of one term.)

At twenty, Cassandra Coleman became the country's youngest female mayor in 2008, when the mayor of Exeter, Pennsylvania, resigned and Coleman was appointed as the new boss. She served

first-time candidates. Depending on your location, these kinds of jobs might be part-time positions where you can, and probably would, work another job or go to school at the same time.

In some races, being young can actually give you an advantage. If you're running against an incumbent who has been around forever, it isn't hard to make the argument that a young candidate brings fresh ideas and a different perspective. For positions that involve working with technology or the education system,

in the job until early 2015, when she left to take a job with the state governor's office.

Also in 2008, John Tyler Hammons was a nineteen-year-old college freshman when he was elected mayor of Muskogee, Oklahoma, defeating a three-term incumbent. After two two-year terms and finishing college, he became an assistant attorney general for the Cherokee Nation. And in 2009, the local council of Sligo, Pennsylvania, unanimously appointed twenty-year-old Jenny Lynn Barger as the borough's mayor.

For the record, you might hear about the "youngest mayor in America" being a little kid, because a handful of small towns hand out the mayor job as an honorary office. As you probably guessed, these honorary titles—called *jovial* titles—don't come with any real power, so they don't count. The mayors listed above actually did things.

Those are just a few recent examples, all from just one office. Otherwise, this list could go on for quite a while.

· ·

someone who recently graduated and works with new devices can have an advantage when talking about these issues during the race.

The bigger the race, the more help you'll probably need with organizing volunteers and raising money. If you want to challenge an incumbent in a party primary, you won't get much help from the party. But win the primary, and you'll probably get that help in the general election.

Even if you lose, or if you have to wait awhile before running for the job you really want, don't let that discourage you. Voters don't necessarily think about this often, but running in (and voting in) down-ballot elections impacts who will eventually run for higher offices.

Look at it this way: even some of the biggest winners in American politics—those who won the presidency—needed to work their way up and to bounce back from early losses. Need proof?

Before Barack Obama was president, he was a US senator from Illinois, and before that a state senator. During his second term in the Illinois legislature, he lost his first federal election, an unsuccessful Democratic primary challenge against incumbent US representative Bobby Rush in 2000. Just four years later, Obama won a close primary for the US Senate, easily won the general election for the seat, and ran for president in another four years.

George W. Bush lost his first political race in 1978, falling six thousand votes shy of a US House seat from Texas. Other than working on his father's campaigns, he didn't go after another government job until 1994, when he successfully ran for governor of Texas, and was reelected to a second term before running for president in 2000.

Bill Clinton, like Bush, also lost his first run for office. In his case, it meant dropping a close 1974 race for a US House seat from Arkansas, but he fared better than previous Democratic candidates for the seat. That gave him the name recognition to win election as the attorney general of Arkansas in 1976, and as governor two years later. He served two separate terms as governor before his 1992 presidential run.

George H. W. Bush had a long résumé before becoming president. His first political job was serving as the Republican Party's county chairman in Harris County, Texas (which includes Houston). He lost a race for his district's House seat in 1964 but won in a different district two years later. Bush lost a Senate race in 1970 (giving up his House seat to run for it), but he went on to serve as ambassador to the United Nations, chairman of the Republican National Committee, envoy to China, director of the CIA, and a two-term vice president, before winning his one term as president in 1988.

If four consecutive presidents could all lose their first elections for the House of Representatives, it's fair to say one loss won't ruin your career. Don't let a fear of losing be the reason you don't go for it.

Section V
After the Election Is Over

We've spent a lot of time talking about elections because they're important, but one last point—the work of government and the life cycle of politics never really end.

Being an informed voter is great, but that doesn't end once all the votes are cast. Elections are how American citizens hire their representatives, but what's more important than who passes the job interview is how they actually perform on the job. The same sources of information we covered in chapter 4 are just as relevant for keeping yourself up to date on what elected officials are saying and doing. Is the president or governor or mayor keeping the promises he or she made during the campaign? What issues are getting priority? What problems have come up that nobody expected during the election, and how are the elected leaders handling them?

Staying informed is part of being a good citizen. It will also help you shoot down crazy arguments at family get-togethers, or with people who pick fights on social media.

There's a saying in politics that every election is also about the next election, and that's worth keeping in mind. If a candidate you liked lost, it might be worth checking in on what they decided to do instead. If they won, and you worked for their campaign, there's a chance that can be a long-term relationship if you want it to be.

As the four presidential careers described in the last section show, any candidate has a chance to work their way up during the course of their career. How voters choose in down-ballot elections helps parties identify candidates worth watching. Nearly every serious contender for president has been either a governor or a senator before going after the top job. There's a good reason for that, as they've had to campaign statewide already. House members, thanks to gerrymandering and local differences, can often be elected without needing to appeal beyond their base (the voters they know will support them). Even the most conservative senator had to campaign in the most liberal part of the state, because getting a slightly higher percentage of the vote there could make enough of a difference to get elected, and the most liberal governor did the same in his or her state's most conservative area.

It's up to voters to evaluate how officials are doing in their current roles, from president down to a part-time local board. All candidates make promises during the campaign, and you can check on whether they at least tried to keep them. The nature of politics is that officials need to compromise (the United States doesn't elect dictators), so nobody's going to be able to pass everything they talked about wanting to do. Still, there's a difference between a mayor, governor, or president who introduced a program they promised but had to compromise with the legislature to get it done (or saw it blocked by opponents in that legislature), and one who made a promise and just ignored it the minute they got elected. It's easy, as the cliché goes, to let the perfect become the enemy of the good. Keep that in mind when you're grading your representatives.

Government is complicated, and officials who actually want to get things done have to know how to negotiate to get laws passed, as well as what can or can't be done by officials in a certain office—but they also need to be able to adapt when new problems come up or old ones return.

During the 2000 election cycle, the presidential candidates barely talked about the threat of terrorism; less than a year after that election, the World Trade Center had been destroyed and polls consistently found terrorism was the issue that citizens were most concerned about. Early in the 2008 election, not many people predicted the country would collapse into the worst recession in almost seventy years. A few weeks before the election, the American economy was in a radically different place, and candidates needed to quickly come up with plans to rebuild it. That's true on smaller scales too. State and local governments were hit hard in the recession (in some cases, harder than the federal government), and candidates probably didn't see that coming when they first got into the race months earlier.

In other words, some of the most important things politicians will do won't necessarily come up in the campaign. While their specific policies are important, voters also need to think about their judgment. Not just the details of their plans, but the thought process behind them. Looking at their track records in office and following how they do their jobs is a pretty good way to gauge how the candidates solve problems.

GETTING IN TOUCH

Following politics is one way to make sure government figures are doing their jobs. Another way is to weigh in on the job itself. For one thing, you can write to your elected officials or call them. It sounds simple, but you might be surprised by how few people do it.

You can e-mail, but honestly, a printed letter in the mail will get more attention. As you probably know from your own life, tweets and posts and e-mails get easily lost in the shuffle. A physical letter, written by someone who put some thought into it, will usually get more attention because it's rare. Also, calls get attention because they mean staffers are talking to a person, while e-mails are less personal and might just sit in an inbox, and social media comments are even easier to ignore. Don't be afraid to tell officials who represent you why you disagree with a stance they're taking or thank them for doing something you support, which is just as important—as with any job, customers complain when they're upset but overlook good service. If there's a vote coming up on an important issue, constituents letting their representatives know how they feel about things can influence that decision. In early 2017, constituent calls in support of the Affordable Care Act played a role in convincing a few key senators to vote against repealing it, saving healthcare coverage for millions of Americans.

To be fair to them, even the most sincere of elected officials (and appointed officials, such as cabinet secretaries) work for a lot of people and have dozens of issues on their plate at any time. Lobbyists and organized movements know this, and they work hard to get some of those officials' limited time. The public should do that too. Even at the local level, any official is supposed to represent his or her constituents, and the constituents who get in touch are going to get more attention than those who don't.

At the federal level, the websites of both the House of Representatives and the Senate list every member of the body, and they have links for each of their individual offices. If you're not sure which House member represents you, the site lets you search by your zip code. The White House website includes links for each of the cabinet departments and executive-branch agencies, along with the big house at 1600 Pennsylvania Avenue.

Don't hesitate to ask your representatives for help if there's something you need that falls within their jurisdiction. Part of any elected official's job is what's known as *constituent services*—helping citizens who have problems with government agencies or have situations for which government intervention might be useful. It isn't just a good way for you to get help; it's part of their job to at least try to assist you or get you more information. Members of the House and Senate have staffers who aid with these services all the time, and there are similar roles in state legislatures. Those staffs have gotten larger in the past few decades (at least on the federal side), and some deal with dozens of constituent cases every month. Your representative's or senator's office can help with questions or concerns involving any federal program, from education grants and student loans to Medicaid and veteran's benefits.

If your grandparents aren't receiving their Social Security checks, their representatives can look into it. If a family is running into paperwork problems adopting a child from another country, a representative's help might make that process easier. It's not unusual for there to be a problem in their home district or state that nobody's ever notified a member of Congress about— say, a farm operation polluting local waters, or a school not being able to get funding it was promised—and just getting them involved can change the outcome. Politicians sometimes run ads about successful constituent-service efforts because they understand that a good story about helping people looks good for them, meaning even the more cynical elected officials have an incentive to help you.

If you're in Washington for any reason, you can also stop by your representatives' offices and talk to them in person. Many senators from both parties have weekly breakfasts while the Senate is in session, where they serve coffee and snacks, talk to constituents about what's going on in DC, and take questions. For some states, the two senators cohost the event; for others, they host on different days. (Some House members do this too.) You can also visit your state legislators in the state capitol. And in both the state and federal cases, you can sometimes watch the legislature in action from the public gallery.

It's worth mentioning that you can watch the work of the judicial branch too. A public trial is a right guaranteed by the Sixth Amendment. There are a few exceptions, if a judge decides that there's a specific public interest in keeping spectators out of the courtroom. Common examples would be rape trials in which the victim's name isn't public or cases that involve classified information. Otherwise, at the federal, state, or local level, you can attend and observe most trials. The public's ability to watch a trial is an important part of keeping the court system open to scrutiny, and watching a trial can be an interesting learning opportunity. Once you're eighteen, you're also eligible to serve on a jury—the right to a trial by an impartial jury being another right guaranteed by the Sixth Amendment.

At the local level, it's even easier to let your representatives know what you think. Boards such as the city council, school board, and zoning board have public meetings, which all constituents can attend. For many local projects—for example, building a mall or raising property taxes—local law will require the city or town to hold a public hearing before work begins. That's a chance for constituents to voice any objections or suggestions they have, and to do it in a public forum, on the record. The specifics differ from place to place, but when government bodies are required to hold a public forum, they're also required to advertise it with enough notice that citizens can plan to attend, in places where citizens have a reasonable chance of seeing the information. Common examples include posting a notice in local newspapers, in government buildings, and on buses or trains.

As we discussed earlier, local government often has a bigger direct impact on your life, even though far fewer people pay attention to it than they do to Washington. That can sometimes lead to corruption and local governments trying to get away with things—ranging from nepotism in hiring to embezzlement of local

"Never doubt that a small group of thoughtful, committed citizens can change the world. Indeed, it is the only thing that ever has."

—AUTHOR AND ANTHROPOLOGIST MARGARET MEAD

tax money—thinking nobody's watching what goes on. The best way to guard against that, of course, is to pay attention and get others to do so too.

On the positive side, public meetings are, by definition, public. If there's something you want the local government to do, bring it up at a meeting when the members ask about new business. Not only will the officials hear what you have to say, but so will other citizens who can serve as potential allies. Just as debates between politicians can give citizens some insight into who to support, hearing citizens debate local policies can give officials insight into how the community feels about present and future priorities. Federal and state agencies hold similar public hearings in areas that will be affected by a policy, and they are required to advertise so that local people can attend. For example, the Environmental Protection Agency may hold public hearings about a cleanup of a local site, or the Department of Defense might hold one about a local base closing. In cases like these, the agency and your individual representatives might agree or disagree. Either way, citizens can let both sides know how they feel.

It's been said for decades (and earlier in this book) that turnout is one of the reasons why issues facing older voters seem to get addressed more frequently than issues facing young voters. But it's not just turnout at elections; it's turnout at meetings, at public hearings, and at community events. To be heard, you often have to go to where people are listening.

WORKING IN THE FIELD

Getting back to the working side of involvement, you can also get a job in politics that focuses on policy rather than on campaigning.

Members of the House and Senate have offices in Washington and in their home state or district, and those offices hire staff. Most government institutions offer internships, which give students or recent graduates a chance to learn on the job. Getting one of those internships can be very competitive, and they can mean long hours without a lot of money (or in some cases, without any), but they're a great foot in the door for a future career in politics.

Just as most officials have full-time staff as well as volunteers during the campaign, most elected and appointed officials have full-time staff members while they're in office. Many of those jobs will be filled by the official's longtime associates, but there are times when jobs open up. Newly elected officials could have more jobs to offer because they won't necessarily have the large existing staff that a veteran official might. Staff jobs can deal with constituent services, communications, policy creation, logistics, or lots of other tasks. You can apply for open positions advertised online. If you have volunteered or worked on a campaign, the contacts you made there can be incredibly helpful in getting a job with an official's office. Professional political operatives often work on many campaigns for different candidates over time, and making a good impression can help your application now and in the future.

Government departments also need employees, from the federal cabinet down to local parks departments and permit offices. Some of these jobs don't focus on creating policies but are an important part of carrying them out. In these roles, you might work closely with elected officials, or you may never interact with the elected side at all. There's probably a role that can make use of whatever skills you have. How well any government department functions has a lot to do with dozens or hundreds of staff members who apply just as they would for any other office job—not just the elected or appointed officials at the top of the organization chart.

Government and nongovernmental organizations also offer short-term or long-term jobs and volunteer opportunities that don't focus on politics but give you a chance to improve society through your work. The Peace Corps is a government-run program through which American volunteers travel abroad to help people in developing countries. AmeriCorps creates full-time and part-time positions to help local communities with civil-service projects. Teach for America is a nonprofit program that places recent college graduates in teaching positions in low-income schools. Those are some of the best-known examples, but there are many others. Nongovernmental and nonprofit organizations, including those mentioned earlier when discussing activism, also have temporary opportunities and full-time jobs in their offices or in the field.

In short, voting is just one of myriad ways to play a role in how government works. Whether it's policy or politics, working inside the system or from the outside, every American has opportunities to be an active citizen.

Section VI
Conclusion

And with that note, congratulations! You've reached the end of the book. The resources section that follows includes some useful resources for getting started on the path to becoming a more involved citizen. (Some, but not all, were mentioned earlier in the book.)

Hopefully, you now have a better understanding of how the US government works, how American citizens elect our leaders, and how you can take part in the process. The country and its system of government aren't perfect, but it's a better system than a lot of others around the world, and it is at its best when more citizens pay attention and get involved. The American system fares better or worse over time, with great leaders and lousy ones, times when government does more for its people and periods when it does less. How that goes down has a lot to do with the choices voters make, both during the election and afterward.

Bill Clinton used to say, "There is nothing wrong with America that cannot be cured by what is right with America." *Nothing* might be a stretch, but a number of problems can be solved if citizens care enough and get engaged. This is still a reasonably young nation, and it has seen much progress since the beginning.

There's always more to do, and we've covered some of the obstacles that stand in the way of change. Two of the biggest obstacles to better government are ignorance and apathy. People who don't know what they're talking about make bad decisions based on bad information, and they're easy to manipulate. People who don't care and opt out leave all the power with others, and there are always people who have bad motivations and care only about getting what they want.

The solution is for more well-meaning Americans to become knowledgeable about government and more interested in politics, and to pass on those qualities until they have numbers on their side. The hope here is that you feel like one of those people. ■

SOURCE NOTES

9   Jeff Fleischer, *Votes of Confidence: A Young Person's Guide to American Elections* (Minneapolis: Zest Books, 2016), 8.

23 "Benjamin Franklin to the Federal Convention," September 17, 1787, *The Founders' Constitution*, Volume 4, Article 7, Document 3, University of Chicago Press, http://press-pubs.uchicago.edu/founders/documents/a7s3.html.

67 "Remarks of Former Vice President Al Gore to the Democratic National Convention," *New York Times*, July 26, 2004, https://www.nytimes.com/2004 /07/26/politics/campaign/remarks-of-former-vice-president-al-gore-to-the -democratic.html.

116 P. J. O'Rourke, *Parliament of Whores: A Lone Humorist Attempts to Explain the Entire U.S. Government* (New York: Grove, 1991).

134 Franklin D. Roosevelt, "Campaign Address from the White House," Franklin D. Roosevelt Presidential Library and Museum, October 4, 1944, http://www.fdrlibrary.marist.edu/_resources/images/msf/msfb0170.

153 Angie Drobnic Holan, "The Media's Definition of Fake News vs. Donald Trump's," PolitiFact, October 18, 2017, https://www.politifact.com/truth -o-meter/article/2017/oct/18/deciding-whats-fake-medias-definition-fake -news-vs/.

154 Hendrik Hertzberg, "Politics and Prose: The Letters of Patrick Moynihan," *New Yorker*, October 18, 2010, https://www.newyorker.com/magazine /2010/10/25/politics-and-prose.

188 Abraham Lincoln, "House Divided Speech," June 16, 1858, Abraham Lincoln Online.org, http://www.abrahamlincolnonline.org/lincoln/speeches/house .htm.

191 Ronald Reagan, "Second Presidential Debate," Commission on Presidential Debates, October 21, 1984, http://content.time.com/time/specials/packages /article/0,28804,1844704_1844706_1844612,00.html.

191 Lloyd Bentsen, "Vice Presidential Debate," Commission on Presidential Debates, October 5, 1988, https://www.debates.org/debate-history/1988 -debates/#oct-5-1988.

191   Joe Biden, "Democratic Presidential Candidates Debate," C-SPAN, October 30, 2007, https://www.c-span.org/video/?201937-1/democratic -presidential-candidates-debate.

191   Barack Obama, "General Election Presidential Debate," Commission on Presidential Debates, October 22, 2012, https://www.debates.org/debate -history/2012-debates/#anchor-four.

192   League of Women Voters, "League Refuses to Help 'Perpetuate a Fraud,'" news release, October 3, 1988, https://www.lwv.org/newsroom/press-releases /league-refuses-help-perpetrate-fraud.

199   Will Rogers, Daily Telegram #1538, "The First Good News of the 1928 Campaign! Mr. Rogers Says He Will Not Run for Anything," June 28, 1931.

240   Nancy C. Lutkehaus, *Margaret Mead: The Making of an American Icon* (Princeton, NJ: Princeton University Press, 2008).

243   William J. Clinton, "First Inaugural Address," January 20, 1993, The Avalon Project at Yale Law School, http://avalon.law.yale.edu/20th_century/clinton1 .asp.

RESOURCES FOR MORE INFORMATION

GOVERNMENT RESOURCES

- Election Assistance Commission: http://www.eac.gov
  Includes resources for voter registration, voter guides, and working at the polls

- Federal Election Commission: http://www.fec.gov
  Includes data for federal campaign financing and the laws surrounding it

- Library of Congress: http://www.loc.gov
  World's largest library, includes searchable records for all books and publications nationwide

- National Conference of States Legislatures: http://www.ncsl.org /research/elections-and-campaigns/ballot-measures-database.aspx
  Includes information about state government around the country, including a searchable historical database of all ballot measures and voter ID requirements

- National Governors Association: http://www.nga.org
  Includes information about all fifty governors and the issues they discuss as a group

- United States Census Bureau: http://www.census.gov
  Includes demographic information for the entire United States population

- United States House of Representatives: http://www.house.gov
  Includes links to every representative's page

- United States Senate: http://www.senate.gov
  Includes links to every senator's page

■ White House: https://www.whitehouse.gov
Information about the president's policies and links to all cabinet and other executive branch offices

NONGOVERNMENT RESOURCES

■ American Civil Liberties Union: https://www.aclu.org
Organization fighting against voter suppression and for numerous rights

■ League of Women Voters Education Fund: http://www.vote411.org
Includes voting registration and information for all states

■ National Constitution Center: http://constitutioncenter.org
Museum devoted to the US Constitution

■ Rock the Vote: http://www.rockthevote.com
Nonpartisan organization focused on young voters, with information on voter registration and volunteer opportunities

■ Run for Something: http://www.runforsomething.net
Political action committee recruiting young people to run for down-ballot offices

NONPARTISAN RESEARCH
ABOUT POLITICS AND ELECTIONS

■ Annenberg Center for Public Policy: http://www.annenbergpublicpolicycenter.org
University of Pennsylvania center known for policy research and analysis

■ Ballotpedia: http://www.ballotpedia.org
Online encyclopedia with information about federal, state, and local elections, including ballot initiatives

■ Center for Responsive Politics: https://www.opensecrets.org
Tracks spending and fund-raising by politicians and outside groups

■ FactCheck.org: http://www.factcheck.org
Site run by Annenberg, fact-checks political claims

- Fair Vote: http://www.fairvote.org
  Nonpartisan voting rights group, includes research and analysis of voting trends

- FiveThirtyEight: http://fivethirtyeight.com
  Site providing statistical analysis of polls and other data

- PolitiFact: http://politifact.com
  Site from the Tampa Bay Times, *fact-checks political claims*

- Poynter: https://www.poynter.org
  Provides fact-checking, as well as analysis of trends in journalism and media

- Snopes: http://www.snopes.com
  Fact-checks urban legends and online rumors

- University of Virginia Center for Politics:
  http://www.centerforpolitics.org
  Nonpartisan civics-education center that publishes research and analysis about politics

- *Washington Post* Fact Checker:
  http://washingtonpost.com/news/fact-checker
  Newspaper site that fact-checks political claims

POLITICAL PARTY ORGANIZATIONS

- Commission on Presidential Debates: http://www.debates.org
  Includes transcripts and, where possible, videos for all presidential debates

- Constitution Party: http://www.constitutionparty.com
  Includes information about the third party, including volunteer opportunities

- Democratic Congressional Campaign Committee: http://dccc.org
  Works to elect Democrats to the US House of Representatives

- Democratic National Committee: https://www.democrats.org
  Includes party platform and volunteer opportunities

- Democratic Senatorial Campaign Committee: http://www.dscc.org
  Works to elect Democrats to the US Senate

- Green Party of the United States: http://www.gp.org
  Includes information about the third party, including volunteer opportunities

- Libertarian National Committee: http://www.lp.org
  Includes information about the third party, including volunteer opportunities

- National Republican Congressional Committee: https://www.nrcc.org
  Works to elect Republicans to the US House of Representatives

- National Republican Senatorial Committee: https://www.nrsc.org
  Works to elect Republicans to the US Senate

- Republican National Committee: https://www.gop.com
  Includes party platform and volunteer opportunities

POLLING FIRMS

- Gallup Organization: http://www.gallup.com
  Includes poll data that can be searched by topic

- Pew Research Center: http://www.pewresearch.org
  Includes poll data that can be searched by topic

- SurveyUSA: http://www.surveyusa.net
  Includes poll data, with most recent polls viewable

- Zogby Analytics: http://www.zogbyanalytics.com
  Includes news releases with recent poll results

INDEX

ABOUT THE AUTHOR

Jeff Fleischer is a Chicago-based author, journalist, and editor. He is the author of the nonfiction books *Rockin' the Boat: 50 Iconic Revolutionaries from Joan of Arc to Malcolm X* and *The Latest Craze: A Brief History of Mass Hysterias*. His work has appeared in dozens of publications including *Mother Jones*, the *Sydney Morning Herald*, *Chicago Magazine*, the *New Republic*, *Mental_Floss*, *National Geographic Traveler*, and the *Chicago Tribune*.

PHOTO ACKNOWLEDGMENTS

Image credits: Harper's Weekly, April 11, 1868/Wikimedia Commons (PD), p. 33; National Board of Review Magazine for November 1939, Volume XIV, Number 8, page 14/Wikimedia Commons (PD), p. 35; CBS Photo Archive/Getty Images, p. 77; Hulton Archive/Getty Images, p. 103; Wikimedia Commons (PD), p. 107; William Thomas Cain/MCT/Getty Images, p. 141; Bettman/Getty Images, p. 189; Rick Friedman/Corbis/Getty Images, p. 209; Independent Picture Service, p. 223.